CHICAGO BICYCLE GUIDEBOOK

Great Bicycle Riding Through Chicago's Lakefront Neighborhoods

MICHAEL PALUCKI

Pastime Publications
Seal Beach, California

Chicago Bicycle Guidebook
Great Bicycle Riding Through Chicago's
Lakefront Neighborhoods
By Michael Palucki

Published by:
Pastime Publications
P.O. Box 3237
Seal Beach, California 90740-2237

Printed in the United States of America

Cover design: Dan Long and Heidi Myers
Cover photos: Dan Broten
Book design and layout: Richard Lyddon

Publisher's Cataloging in Publication Data

Palucki, Michael,
Chicago Bicycle Guidebook.

Includes index,
1. Chicago (IL) - Description - Bicycle Tours.
2. Bicycle Touring - Chicago, Illinois,
3. Chicago - Description and travel - Guidebooks.

Library of Congress Catalog Card Number: 92-085158
ISBN: 0-9634829-7-1

First Printing, 1993

Acknowledgments

I want to thank the many people who assisted in the writing and production of this book. Chicago Bicycle Federation members Mike Erikson and Larry O'Toole offered early encouragement to the idea of a Chicago bicycle guidebook. Russell Lewis, of the Chicago Historical Society, reviewed the manuscript for historical accuracy. Copy editor Steve Stelpflug reviewed the manuscript and provided excellent advise. Dan Broten provided expert photography and rode along on several of the routes. Don and Sharon Brundige, along with Ed Zolkoski, shared their experiences in guidebook production.

Additionally, many people were helpful with their positive attitude and enthusiastic support. Jeff Tanaka, Helen Salazar, Tom Griffin, Bill Peirsol, Tom O'Malley, Michael Torney, Bob Spran, my sisters Debbie and Teddie, brother Jeff, and, of course, Mary and Ted Palucki (mom and dad) were always there with helpful encouragement. I thank you all.

Finally, there is one person whose contribution is beyond measurement - my wife Marge Salazar. Her positive attitude and resourceful ways were instrumental in keeping me going, and without her this book could not have been written.

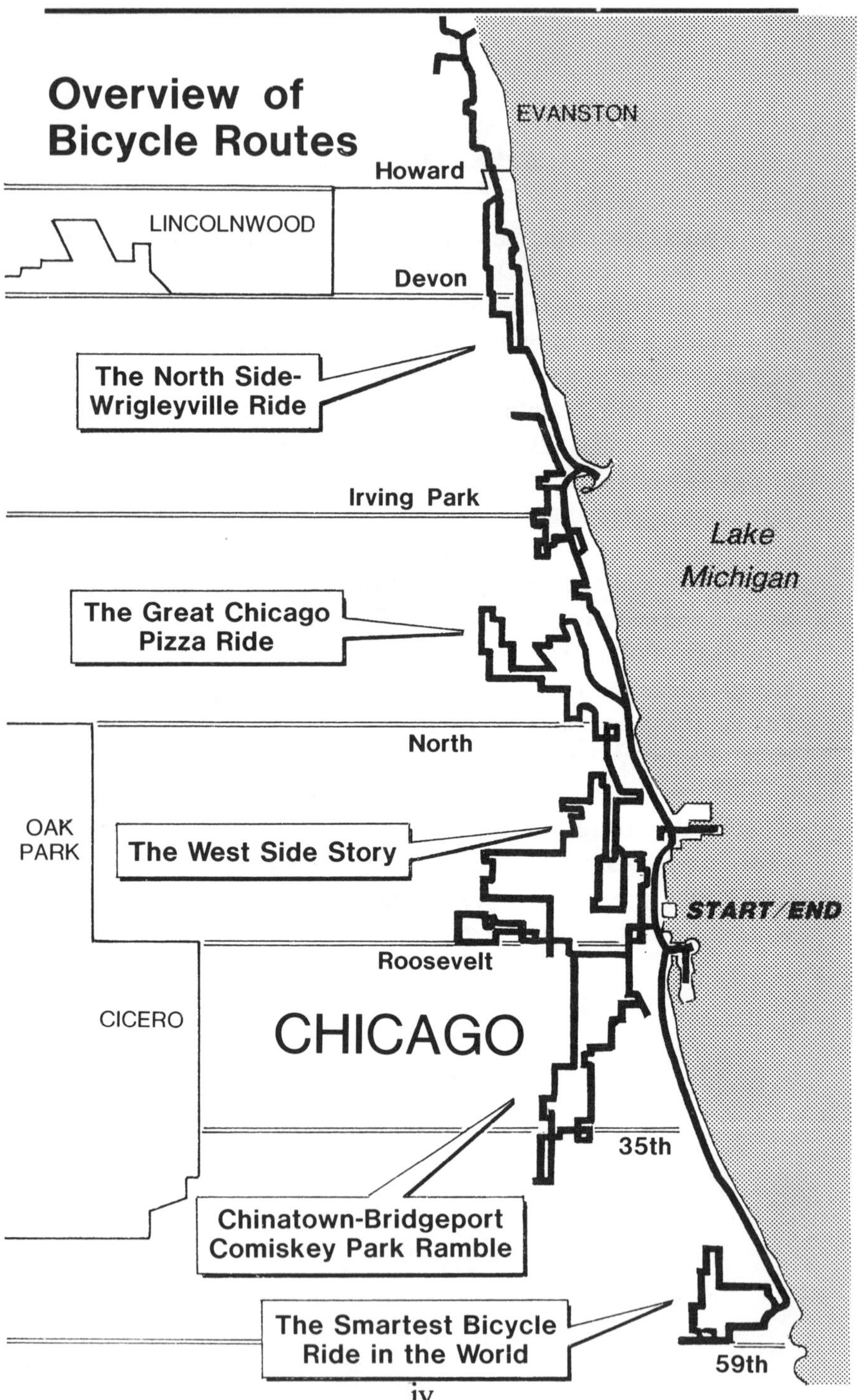
Overview of Bicycle Routes
EVANSTON
Howard
LINCOLNWOOD
Devon
The North Side-Wrigleyville Ride
Irving Park
Lake Michigan
The Great Chicago Pizza Ride
North
OAK PARK
The West Side Story
START/END
Roosevelt
CICERO
CHICAGO
35th
Chinatown-Bridgeport Comiskey Park Ramble
The Smartest Bicycle Ride in the World
59th

TABLE OF CONTENTS

Introduction **1**

A Quick Use Guide **3**

General Information **4**

Arrival and Parking 4
Bicycle Rental and Equipment 4
Using the Maps 5
Bicycle Safety and Crime 5

How To Use This Book **7**

I. Chinatown-Bridgeport - Comiskey Park Ramble 11
A. Stockyard Gate Loop 20

II. The Great Chicago Pizza Ride **27**
A. Wrightwood and Lakeview Loop 39

III. The Smartest Bicycle Ride in the World **47**
A. Solidarity Drive Loop 54
B. Japanese Garden Loop 62

IV. The West Side Story **65**
A. "Loop" Loop 71
B. Union Park and Jackson Boulevard Loop 76
C. West Side Medical Center Loop 79
D. Maxwell Street Market Loop 80

V. The North Side-Wrigleyville Ride **83**
A. Graceland Cemetery Loop 93
B. Little Saigon Loop 94
C. Loyola and Northwestern University Loop . 95

For More Information **103**

Recommended Reading **104**

Index **106**

Warning - Disclaimer

Pastime Publications, the author, and all other individuals involved in the making of this guidebook, shall have neither liability nor responsibility to any person with respect to property damage, bodily injury, or death, caused, or alleged to be caused, directly or indirectly by the information contained in this book. Pastime Publications in no way guarantees the safety or fitness of the recommended routes. Cycling is a sport that can be dangerous and no guidebook can alert you to every hazard. Traffic signs along the route and actual road conditions take precedence over the information contained in this guidebook.

Introduction

For most Chicago-area cyclists, cycling in the city consists of a regular pilgrimage along Chicago's Lakefront Bicycle Path. There's a good reason for this enjoyable routine, as there are few urban bicycle rides as beautiful or impressive as the 18 miles of park land along Chicago's stretch of Lake Michigan. Fortunately, there are other interesting and beautiful rides in Chicago, the best of which are covered in this guidebook. In fact, Chicago Bicycle Guidebook will introduce a new approach to cycling in the city - an approach that includes the Lakefront Bicycle Path as well as the best of Chicago's famous neighborhoods. Bicycle routes include: The Chinatown-Bridgeport-Comiskey Park Ramble; The Great Chicago Pizza Ride; The Smartest Bicycle Ride in the World; The West Side Story; and The North Side-Wrigleyville Ride.

Though Chicago-area residents bicycle more than the national average, Chicago is generally not considered among the top bicycling cities in America. Unlike recognized cycling-friendly cities such as Boulder, Colorado, or San Diego, California, the streets of Chicago were designed to meet the needs of factories and workers who ran them, not to satisfy the recreational needs of post industrial babyboomers. Author Norman Mailer once called Chicago, "the last of the great American cities." The city's authenticity stems from an unpretentious past rooted in the nation's heartland. What Chicago lacks in natural wonders it more than makes up for with historic, architecturally significant, culturally diverse, and exciting urban neighborhoods. If driving through Chicago's Loop or Michigan Avenue is exciting - cruising it on a bicycle is absolutely exhilarating!

The bicycle routes in the Chicago Bicycle Guidebook are laid out in circular loops that begin and end near Buckingham

Fountain in Grant Park. By starting and ending in the heart of the city, cyclists get the combined thrill of Chicago's central cityscape as well as the more tranquil, and perhaps "real," Chicago as seen through its unique ethnic neighborhoods. Depending upon optional sidetrips and shortcuts, the bicycle routes range in length from 6.5 miles to 37.7 miles. Each circular loop can be shortened or lengthened to suit the rider's ability and time constraints.

Each ride includes a route map detailing the streets and attractions along the way. Because much of Chicago's character lies in its ethnic past, each ride narrative also includes a brief historical perspective. There are also sections highlighting the cultural and recreational attractions along the route, as well as nearby bicycle shops. Finally, where appropriate, dining and drinking suggestions (all ethnically authentic Chicago) are also provided. Each ride in this guidebook has been personally essayed, and with each visit to the neighborhoods my admiration for the city has increased tremendously. I hope your cycling experiences will bring you even greater rewards.

Midwest Buddhist Temple - M. Palucki

A Quick Use Guide

Because everyone's interest and motivation for cycling is different, there are three recommended ways to use this guidebook. Choose the one that best meets your needs.

1. <u>Read Now - Ride Later</u>

   a. Read "General Information"
   b. Read "How To Use This Book"
   c. Select route and read each section
   d. Read the descriptive narrative
   e. Review the map(s)
   f. Go for a ride

2. <u>Read - Ride - Read More Later</u>

   a. Read "Bicycle Safety and Crime"
   b. Select route and read each section
   c. Review the map(s)
   d. Go for a ride
   e. Read the descriptive narrative

3. <u>Ride Now - Read Later</u>

   a. Read "Bicycle Safety and Crime"
   b. Review desired route map(s)
   c. Go for a ride
   d. Maybe read the book later

General Information

Arrival and Parking

Each route begins and ends at the intersection of Columbus Drive and Monroe Drive in Grant Park, located one block west of Lake Shore Drive, two blocks north of Buckingham Fountain.

The Chicago Park District Monroe Drive underground parking facility is located just north of Monroe Drive on Columbus Drive. Cyclists with roof racks **be aware** that the underground parking lot has a 6'8" clearance. Parking fees at this lot are less than at nearby private parking facilities. As an alternative, you can park at any of the metered spaces in and around Grant Park; in the Chicago Park District parking lots near Soldier Field and McCormick Place at Lake Shore Drive between Roosevelt Road (12th Street) and Cermak Road (22nd Street); or on the street or in the private parking facilities south of Congress Parkway and west of Michigan Avenue.

Bicycle Rentals

Turin Bicycles
435 E. Illinois Street
(312) 923-0100

Erehwon Mountain Supply
644 N. Orleans Street
(312) 337-6400

Village Cycle Center
1337 North Wells Street
(312) 751-2488

These are full service bicycle shops offering quality equipment and are within a few minutes drive from the "Loop."

Equipment

Though traveling light is always recommended, some things are a must for every cyclist. These include:

- Helmet
- Water bottle
- Small tool kit that contains a set of tire irons, a patch kit, a spare tube, adjustable wrench, and screwdriver
- Frame mounted air pump
- Fold up Chicago street map
- Chicago Bicycle Guidebook
- Money for food or emergencies
- Quality U-Lock and/or cable

Using the Maps

Each bicycle route includes a map(s) outlining the designated route. The map(s) show the location for nearby attractions. Those unfamiliar with the area should bring along a Chicago street map for reference.

Bicycle Safety

To the leisure rider, cycling in the large city looks a lot more dangerous than it really is. However, with some common sense rules and a little experience, anyone can pedal through traffic like a hardened veteran. Fortunately, most of the rides in this guidebook are on residential streets or off-road bicycle paths where the riding conditions are quite pleasant.

Taking young children along, either on their own bicycles or in a child seat, should depend on the cyclist's riding ability. The routes along the Lakefront Bicycle Path are fine for children, though these routes are much safer on weekdays. The routes through the neighborhoods at times pass along commercial sections or cross busy streets; therefore, only cyclists with advanced riding skills are recommended to ride these routes.

Listed below are some basic rules of the road for all cyclists.

- Obey all traffic laws as if you were driving a car.
- Always ride on the right side and ***never*** ride against traffic.
- Wear light clothing, reflective vests, and other gear to increase your visibility to motorists.
- Be predictable by riding in a straight line and always use hand signals when turning.
- Be alert for suddenly-opened car doors and cars pulling into traffic from the curb.
- ***Always*** wear a helmet! It has been found that 75% of bicycle fatalities are from head injuries.
- Keep your bicycle in good working order - check your brakes carefully before each ride.
- If night riding use red rear reflectors and a headlight on the front.
- Yield to pedestrians and never challenge cars; in an accident, they will win every time.
- Ride with **CONFIDENCE.** You have a legal right to the roadway and you may use as much of the lane as needed to ride safely.

Crime

The routes in Chicago Bicycle Guidebook include Chicago's most popular and unique areas. Statistics show that these are among the safest neighborhoods in the city. To further ensure a safe ride, avoid potential problems by being prepared: know your route, ride only in daylight, ride with a partner, be alert, trust your instincts - if someone looks dangerous then move on - and most of all, ride with confidence and you can project that you belong and are not to be bothered.

Always carry a bicycle lock when going for a ride in order to prevent bicycle theft. One way to play it safe, since most thieves don't carry two sets of crime tools, is to use both a U-lock and a cable lock. The bottom line is lock your bicycle wisely.

How To Use This Book

The headings at the beginning of each bicycle route are designed to help you plan your ride. These include:

Start/End

Each route in this book begins and ends at the intersection of Columbus Drive and Monroe Drive, in the heart of Grant Park.

Distance

The distance listed is the round trip mileage with notation for shortcuts or optional sidetrips.

Time

The time given is an approximation and was calculated making only an occasional stop.

Difficulty/Safety

Easy rides are under 14 miles, moderate rides between 14 and 20 miles, and strenuous rides over 20 miles. Traffic volume along residential streets is rated light, commercial streets are moderate, and busy thruways are heavy.

Shortcuts

This section lists shortcuts and the mileage saved by using them.

Sidetrips

If applicable, a list of optional sidetrips is provided along with mileage for each sidetrip.

Bicycle Shops

The name, address, and phone number for nearby bicycle shops are listed at the beginning of each ride.

Activities/Highlights

This section includes the name, address, and phone number for attractions along the route. Refer to this section when planning the time frame for your trip.

Dan Broten

Chinatown-Bridgeport Comiskey Park Ramble

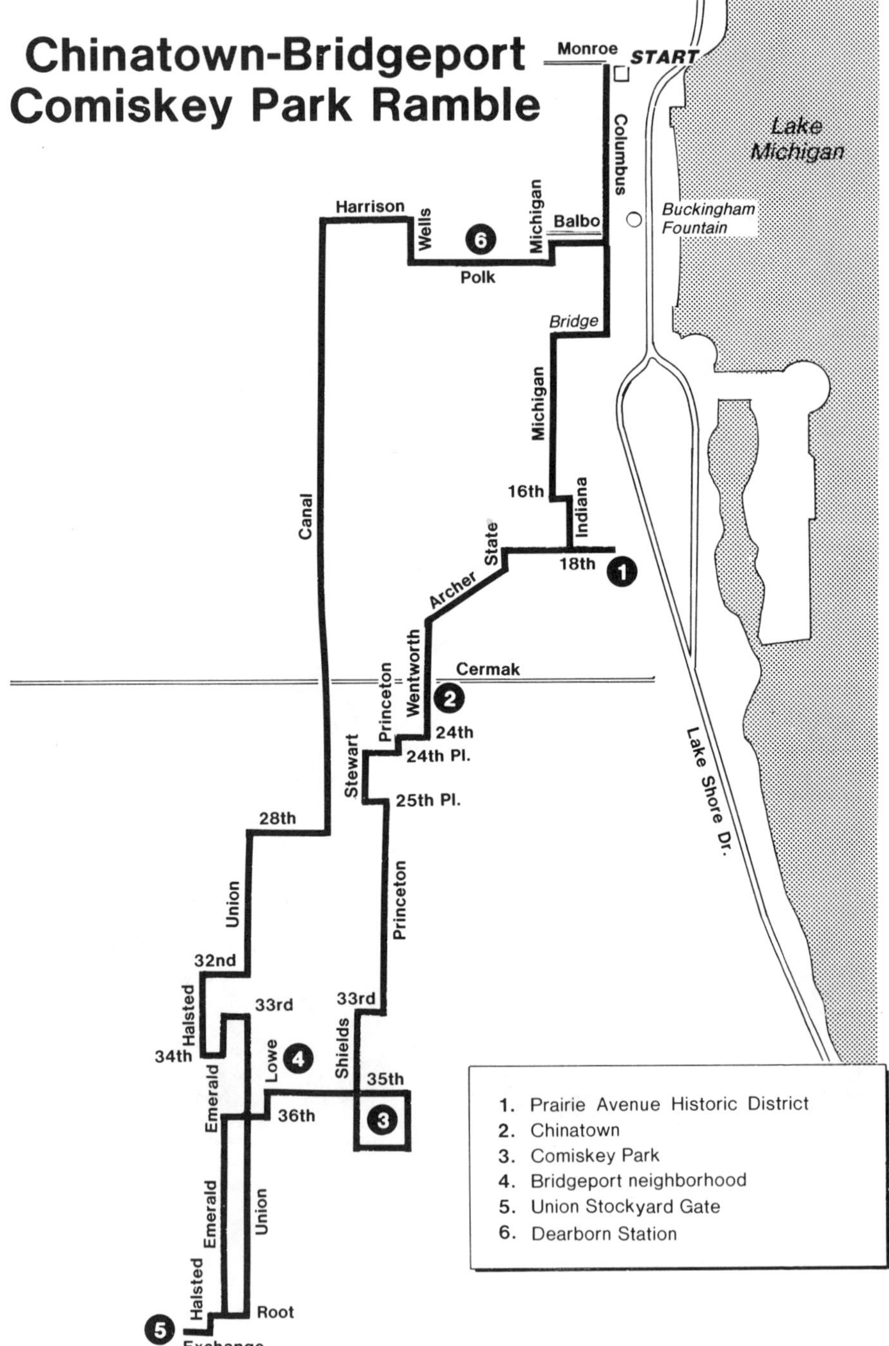

1. Prairie Avenue Historic District
2. Chinatown
3. Comiskey Park
4. Bridgeport neighborhood
5. Union Stockyard Gate
6. Dearborn Station

Chinatown-Bridgeport- Comiskey Park Ramble

Start/End: Intersection of Columbus Drive and Monroe Drive

Distance: 13.7 miles (shortcut reduces ride to 11.7 miles)

Time: 2-3 hours depending on sight-seeing and other stops

Difficulty/Safety: Easy distance
Moderate traffic conditions

Shortcut: Skip Union Stockyard Gate Loop and save 2 miles

Bicycle Shops: Kozy's Cyclery/Fitness
1610 W. 35th Street
(at Ashland Ave.)
(312) 523-8576

Activities/Highlights

Prairie Avenue Historic District
1800 S. Prairie Avenue
(312) 922-3432

Chicago's Chinatown
Wentworth Avenue and Cermak Road (22nd Street)

Comiskey Park - Home of the Chicago White Sox
35th Street and Shields Avenue

Neighborhoods of Armour Square and Bridgeport

Union Stockyard Gate - Historic Landmark
Exchange Avenue just west of Halsted Street

Dearborn Station - Historic Landmark
Polk Street and Dearborn Street

South Loop - M. Palucki

River City in South Loop - M. Palucki

Chinatown-Bridgeport-Comiskey Park Ramble

"Is it the fault of Chicago that the world is carnivorous."
William Archer, "America Today" (1899)

"...Hog Butcher for the World, Tool Maker, Stacker of Wheat,
Player with Railroads and the Nation's Freight Handler;
Stormy, husky, brawling, City of the Big Shoulders...."
Carl Sandburg, Chicago (1916)

The Chinatown-Bridgeport-Comiskey Park Ramble is perhaps the most favored ride in this guidebook. The neighborhoods seem to capture many of Chicago's contrasting elements including its beautiful lakefront parks and vacant industrial scapes; peaceful residential streets and aging commercial avenues; a multi-million dollar baseball stadium with aging high-rise public housing as a backdrop; modern sleekly curved elevated public transit lines and rusting historic iron bridges. Amazingly, all of this is within a 13 mile ride.

The route officially winds through four Chicago neighborhoods: Near South Side, Armour Square, Bridgeport and South Loop. However, within these neighborhoods are other sub-neighborhoods such as the Prairie Avenue Historic District, Chinatown, Canal Street Corridor, and Printers Row - all of which have their own distinct boundaries and ethnicity.

The ride begins in the heart of Grant Park at the intersection of Columbus and Monroe Drive. This area, which has emerged as

Chicago's summertime front yard, annually hosts the largest, most popular, and critically acclaimed civic events in the city. See "The Smartest Bicycle Ride In the World" chapter for a discussion on Grant Park's early history.

Riding south along Columbus Drive (stay on the east side pedestrian/bicycle sidewalk) you pass the James C. Petrillo Music Shell. Throughout the summer this is the site of Chicago's popular free music festivals; The Blues Festival, The Taste of Chicago, The Chicago Jazz Festival, and evening concerts by the Grant Park Symphony Orchestra. Directly across from the music shell, on the west side of Columbus Drive, is the School of the Art Institute and behind the school is the Art Institute of Chicago.

Buckingham Fountain - Dan Broten

When crossing Jackson Drive, you will see the beautiful Clarence Buckingham Fountain. Donated to the city in 1927, Buckingham Fountain (as it is popularly known) immediately became the central focus point of all of Grant Park. It would be a rare exception for a true Chicagoan's photo album to not contain at least one family picture in front of the fountain. According to author Ira Bach, in the Guide to Chicago's Public Sculpture, the four identical pairs of bronze sea horses placed in the fountain pools symbolize the four states that border Lake Michigan.

Continuing south on Columbus Drive, you will cross Congress Parkway and Balboa Drive. On the south side of Balboa Drive, cross Columbus Drive and continue south on the marked sidewalk/ bicycle path (along the west side of Columbus Drive). This area is lined with several ballfields and tennis courts, and includes a nice view of the shimmering lake (on your left) and Chicago's magnificent skyline (on your right). One quarter mile south of Balboa Drive, on your right, is the marked pedestrian/bicycle bridge over the Illinois Central railroad tracks. Follow the path across the bridge to Michigan Avenue. The total distance from the starting point is one mile.

The ride has entered the Near South Side. Today, the Near South Side is primarily a commercial area comprised of old warehouses and empty store fronts. In 1837, when Chicago was incorporated as a city, the Near South Side was uninhabited marsh land - though not without a colorful history. During the War of 1812, Fort Dearborn (the original settlement of Chicago) was ordered abandoned. As soldiers and settlers fled they were ambushed in this vicinity by Indians. This has since been known as the Fort Dearborn Massacre.

As Chicago grew southward from its central business district, the Near South Side became increasingly popular as commercial and residential area. The Chicago Fire of 1871 did not burn this section of the city, therefore, much of the post fire growth occurred here.

From the pedestrian/bicycle bridge to Chinatown, follow the designated route. The first destination is the Prairie Avenue Historic District just one mile from the pedestrian/bicycle bridge. Take Michigan Avenue south to 16th Street. Make a left turn and go east one block to Indiana Avenue. At Indiana Avenue make a right turn, go south to 18th Street. At 18th Street turn left and travel east one block to Prairie Avenue and the historic district. Just before Prairie Avenue (on your right) is the Glessner House Bookstore and the commemorative plaques highlighting the history and facts about the area.

As Chicago was experiencing its post-fire building spree a small section of the Near South Side along Prairie Avenue, between 16th and 22nd Streets, became home to the richest and most powerful people in Chicago. The aristocracy of Chicago spent their fortunes on mansions, and turned this section of town into a virtual museum of residential architecture. George M. Pullman (maker of railway sleeper cars), Philip D. Armour of meat-packing fame, A. Montgomery Ward of the mail order retail trade, William Kimball the piano and organ builder, Marshall Field Jr. (retail maverick), and Potter Palmer (real estate tycoon) were just a few of Chicago's gilded agers to build and live along Prairie Avenue. By the late 19th century the Near South Side became more commercial and was less attractive to Chicago's wealthy. By the turn of the century many of the residents along Prairie Avenue had moved north to Astor Street in Lincoln Park.

Leaving the Prairie Avenue Historic District, travel .9 mile to the intersection of Wentworth Avenue and Cermak Road (22nd Street). Take 18th Street west, past Indiana Avenue, Michigan Avenue, Wabash Avenue and finally to State Street. This general vicinity was the headquarters for the Al Capone criminal organization. The Lexington Hotel, at 1825 S. Michigan Ave. was Capone headquarters from 1928 to 1932. Capone also controlled several floors of the Metropole Hotel which was located at 2300 S. Michigan Avenue. Since the Metropole Hotel has been demolished and the Lexington Hotel is barely standing, neither site was included in the route.

At State Street, you find yourself directly under the Lake-Dan Ryan El line. Make a left turn onto State Street and go south one-half block to the traffic light at Archer Avenue. At Archer Avenue go right and continue in a southwest direction past Clark Street (disregard the posted Chinatown direction sign), under the railroad tracks, and make a left turn onto the first street west of the railroad tracks which is southbound Wentworth Avenue. Looking south from Archer Avenue you will notice the cylindrical shaped mid-rise apartment towers located at Cermak Road (22nd St.) and State Street. These are the Raymond Hilliard Homes, a public housing project, designed by Bertrand Goldberg who also designed Marina City and River City.

Continuing south on Wentworth Avenue and as you cross Cermak Road, you enter Chicago's Chinatown. Most of the restaurants and shops are located on Cermak Road and Wentworth Avenue, with the surrounding streets residential. Chinatown is actually the northern section of the Armour Square neighborhood. Armour Square, which takes its name from a small park located at 34th Street and Shields Avenue, is unique in that its physical boundaries are shaped by transportation corridors. The northern boundary is roughly the elevated portion of the Dan Ryan express-way. The west end of the neighborhood is bordered by the Chicago and Western Indiana rail lines and on the eastern edge, the Chicago, Rock Island, and Pacific rail lines serve as a marker. The southern boundary is roughly Comiskey Park and the nearby parking lots. The result is a 4-5 block wide neighborhood that runs from 19th Street to 39th Street.

The ride leaves Chinatown along Wentworth Avenue south to 24th Street. Go right on 24th Street and continue west one block to to Princeton Avenue. On the northwest corner of 24th Street and Princeton Avenue is Bertucci's Corners, a delightful neighborhood Italian restaurant which has been featured many times as one of Chicago's "hidden gems" of restaurants. This section of Armour Square has traditionally been Italian and many still live here.

Make a left and travel south on Princeton Avenue to 24th Place. Go right on 24th Place and proceed to Stewart Avenue. At Stewart Avenue, just east of the Chicago and Western Indiana Railroad tracks, make a left turn and go south across the Stevenson Expressway and make a left turn onto 25th Place. Make a right turn onto Princeton Avenue and follow it south to 26th Street where Princeton Avenue jogs to the left.

Traveling south on Princeton Avenue places you in the heart of Armour Square. Armour Square has been linked historically to the Bridgeport neighborhood, although many Chicagoans wouldn't know that there is a distinction. Working class Irish followed by Germans, Swedes, Italians, Croations, Chinese, African-Americans, and Mexicans have all called Armour Square home.

Traveling south, cross 31st Street which is the main commercial street for Armour Square. At 33rd Street and Princeton you will see Armour Square Park, and just beyond Armour Square Park, looming up like a giant futuristic mushroom, is the new Comiskey Park. Jimbo's Lounge, on the northwest corner of Princeton and 33rd Street, is a popular local watering hole - especially on White Sox game days.

Go right on 33rd Street to Shields Avenue, then make a left and go south to the ballpark. If modern stadiums interest you, take a ride around the perimeter of the new ballpark. Completed in time for the Chicago White Sox home opener on April, 18, 1991, the new Comiskey Park replaces the original Comiskey Park, which was known as the "Baseball Palace of the World," when it opened on July 1, 1910. The old park was located across 35th street and was site of many of baseball's "greatest" moments, including, the first and last midget ever to bat in the majors (he walked, by the way), the first exploding scoreboard, and the first game ever forfeited by the home team because of a disco demolition riot. The scandal plagued 1919 Chicago "Black Sox", led by the immortal "Shoeless" Joe Jackson, played at the old Comiskey. Baseball greatness seems to have eluded the White Sox. In 1959 the White Sox lost the World Series to the Dodgers and on the inauguration of the new Comiskey Park they lost to the Detroit Tigers 16 to 0.

The old Comiskey Park - Dan Broten

Total distance from the starting point to Comiskey Park is 5.3 miles. The route continues by traveling westbound on 35th street and as you pass under the Chicago and Western Indiana Railroad tracks (use street or sidewalk) you enter Bridgeport. Bridgeport is one of Chicago's oldest neighborhoods and its most politically powerful. Settled by working class Irish who came to dig the Illinois & Michigan Canal, Bridgeport has also been home to Germans, Poles, Lithuanians, Native Americans, and Mexican-Americans. The neighborhood is named for a low bridge that spanned the south branch of the Chicago River at Ashland Avenue. In the 1840's barges heading for Chicago couldn't pass under the bridge, and, therefore, had to be unloaded and then reloaded on the other side of the "port."

Continue west on 35th Street and make a left onto Lowe Avenue. About halfway down the block, on the west side of the street, is the home of the late Mayor Richard J. Daley. Bridgeport's domination of Chicago's mayoral post and political scene began with Mayor Ed Kelly (1933-1947), followed by Mayor Martin Kennelly (1947-1955), Mayor Richard J. Daley (1955-1976), Mayor Michael Bilandic (1976-1977), and current Mayor Richard M. Daley.

Union Stockyard Gate Loop

Next its on to the Union Stockyard Gate. To shortcut the Union Stockyard Gate Loop simply go right on 36th Street to Union Avenue and make a right. The designated route goes right on 36th street to Emerald Avenue. At Emerald Avenue make a left and proceed south less than one mile to the Stockyard Gate located at Exchange Avenue (approximately 42nd Street) and Halsted Street.

Once crossing over Pershing Road (39th Street) you will have left Bridgeport and entered the Canaryville neighborhood. Stay south on Emerald and pass under the railroad viaduct. Watch for glass, cracks, and pot holes. At Root Street go right and continue west for one block to Halsted Street. Cross Halsted Street at the light and jog slightly to the left and pickup westbound Exchange Avenue.

The Union Stockyard Gate is just west of Halsted Street on Exchange Avenue. At the gate you will have peddled a total of 6.9 miles from the starting point in Grant Park.

As you peddle west on Exchange Avenue you see the Union Stockyard Gate - one of the only surviving reminders of the once sprawling meat processing complex known as the Union Stockyards. The gate was designed by one of Chicago's premier architectural firms, Burnham & Root, and was erected in 1875. Standing near the gate and looking south and west it's hard to imagine that upwards of fifty thousand workers once toiled at the unsavory task of slaughtering and butchering cattle, calves, hogs, and sheep. At its peak during the 1920s, this complex was the largest of its type in the world.

Adjacent to the Stockyards was infamous "Packing Town," where thousands of newly arrived immigrants were employed in some of the most brutal and unsafe working conditions imaginable. Author Upton Sinclair's harrowing novel The Jungle, published in 1906, chronicles the horrors, disease, poverty and despair of a young Lithuanian immigrant who went to work in one of the packing houses. So moving was Sinclair's novel that it led to government investigations of the packing houses and eventual passage of pure food laws.

With completion of the interstate highway system and the emergence of the trucking industry, the fate of Chicago's Union Stockyards were sealed. By the early 1960s most of the major meat-packers had pulled out, and on August 1, 1971, the Union Stockyards closed forever.

Return to Bridgeport by back tracking on Exchange Avenue, Root Street, and finally to Union Avenue (2 blocks east of Halsted Street). At Union Avenue go left and continue north crossing Pershing Road (39th Street) and re-enter the Bridgeport neighborhood. It is approximately 1.5 miles from the Stockyard Gate to the home of current Mayor Richard M. Daley.

Continue north on Union Avenue, passing the many brick and frame two-flats, corner grocery stores, and an occasional neighborhood tavern. On the southeast corner of Union Avenue and 35th Street is Morrie O'Malley's Hot Dog stand - carrying on a long tradition of Chicago's famous "Chicago Style Hot Dog." Hot Dogs are serious business in Chicago. There are over 2,000 Hot Dog stands in the metropolitan area.

Continue north on Union Avenue and make a left at 33rd Street. Go west one block to Emerald Avenue and make a another left turn. About one-third of the way down the block on your right you'll see Mayor Richard M. Daley's home. Continue to the corner and make a right onto 34th Street to Halsted Street. Make a right on Halsted Street and continue north to 32nd Street.

Halsted Street, along with 31st Street, is the major commercial street serving Bridgeport. The ethnic diversity of this neighborhood can be seen by the restaurants lining Halsted Street between 34th and 32nd Streets. Mexican taco stands, Italian pizza parlors, Chinese fast food, a French pastry shop, and a Lithuanian restaurant are just a few of the eating establishments found here.

Make a right onto 32nd Street, go two blocks east to Union Avenue. At Union Avenue go left and continue north to 28th Street. Go right at 28th Street and follow it east four blocks to Canal Street.

At 28th Street and Canal Street you will have cycled 1.4 miles from the Mayor's home and a total of 9.7 miles from the starting point. Begin your return to the starting point by going left on Canal Street and heading north 2.2 miles to the United States Post Office at Canal Street and Harrison Street. The Canal Street corridor represents the urban adventure portion of the route, in that you will ride through an aging industrial and commercial area that offers sights, sounds, and smells of an almost bygone era - "Chicago as the transportation and industrial center of America."

Just south of 27th Street you pass under the Dan Ryan Expressway and then over the Stevenson Expressway. Further north, near Cermak Road, you pass under the Chicago Transit

Authority Midway Airport elevated transit line. Continuing, cross the Chicago River and you will see aging rusted bridges and other remnants of the industries that were once at work here.

Just south along the river is where the Illinois & Michigan Canal began its 120 mile route to Peru, Illinois. Crossing the river you can see the Burlington Northern rail yards and storage areas for Amtrak passenger trains. Thousands of suburbanites pass through this industrial wasteland daily as they ride comfortable commuter rail cars into downtown Chicago. In less than a two mile stretch of Canal Street you can see Chicago's dynamism as a transportation center: expressways, railroad lines, the Chicago River, an elevated public transit line, and now, a bicycle route.

Dan Broten

On the northeast corner of Canal Street and Harrison Street is the United States Post Office said to be the largest postal facility under one roof in the world. Make a right on Harrison Street and continue east crossing the Chicago River and make a right turn at Wells Street. Crossing the river you can see Bertrand Goldberg's River City complex to the south. This beautiful upscale apartment and marina complex is part of the on-going gentrification of the South Loop neighborhood. River City is located at 800 South Wells Street. If you have a few minutes wander into River City and check out the marina, health club, and views of the rail yards and vacant industrial sites.

After leaving River City, take Polk Street east (watch for pot holes, glass, and other debris as you cross under the railroad viaduct). The numerous restaurants and trendy bars are all relatively new and part of the general upswing in residential development since 1980. As you near LaSalle Street, you will see the gleaming clock tower of Dearborn Station which marks the heart of the Printers Row Historic District. Many of the large buildings just north of the station used to house Chicago's burgeoning printing industry. The printers left and now "rehabbers" have turned these handsome skyscrapers into highly desirable rentals, condos, and lofts.

The Dearborn Station is the oldest surviving metropolitan rail terminal in the United States. Opened on May 1, 1885 the Romanesque Revival terminal with its 170-foot clock tower was the state of the art passenger rail facility of its time. At its peak, the terminal handled hundreds of daily arrivals and departures, and thousands of passengers. The last passenger train pulled into Dearborn Station on May 2, 1971, thereby closing an era in American transportation history. In 1986 the Dearborn Station was completely renovated and turned into a mixed-use shopping facility.

After leaving Dearborn Station, it is approximately one mile to the starting point at Monroe Drive and Columbus Drive. Continue east on Polk Street until it ends at State Street. At State Street go left and pedal a short distance to Balboa Drive, then make a right and continue east. Looking north on State Street you can see the Harold Washington Public Library at State Street and Congress Parkway. On your immediate left is the Pacific Garden Mission serving Chicago's needy and homeless.

Traveling east on Balboa Drive, you cross Michigan Avenue and enter Grant Park. Stay on Balboa Drive and cross Columbus Drive. On the east side of Columbus Drive take the pedestrian/bicycle sidewalk north along Columbus Drive and return to Monroe Drive. Should you wish to ride the Lakefront Bicycle Path take Balboa Drive, Jackson Drive, or Monroe Drive east and cross Lake Shore Drive.

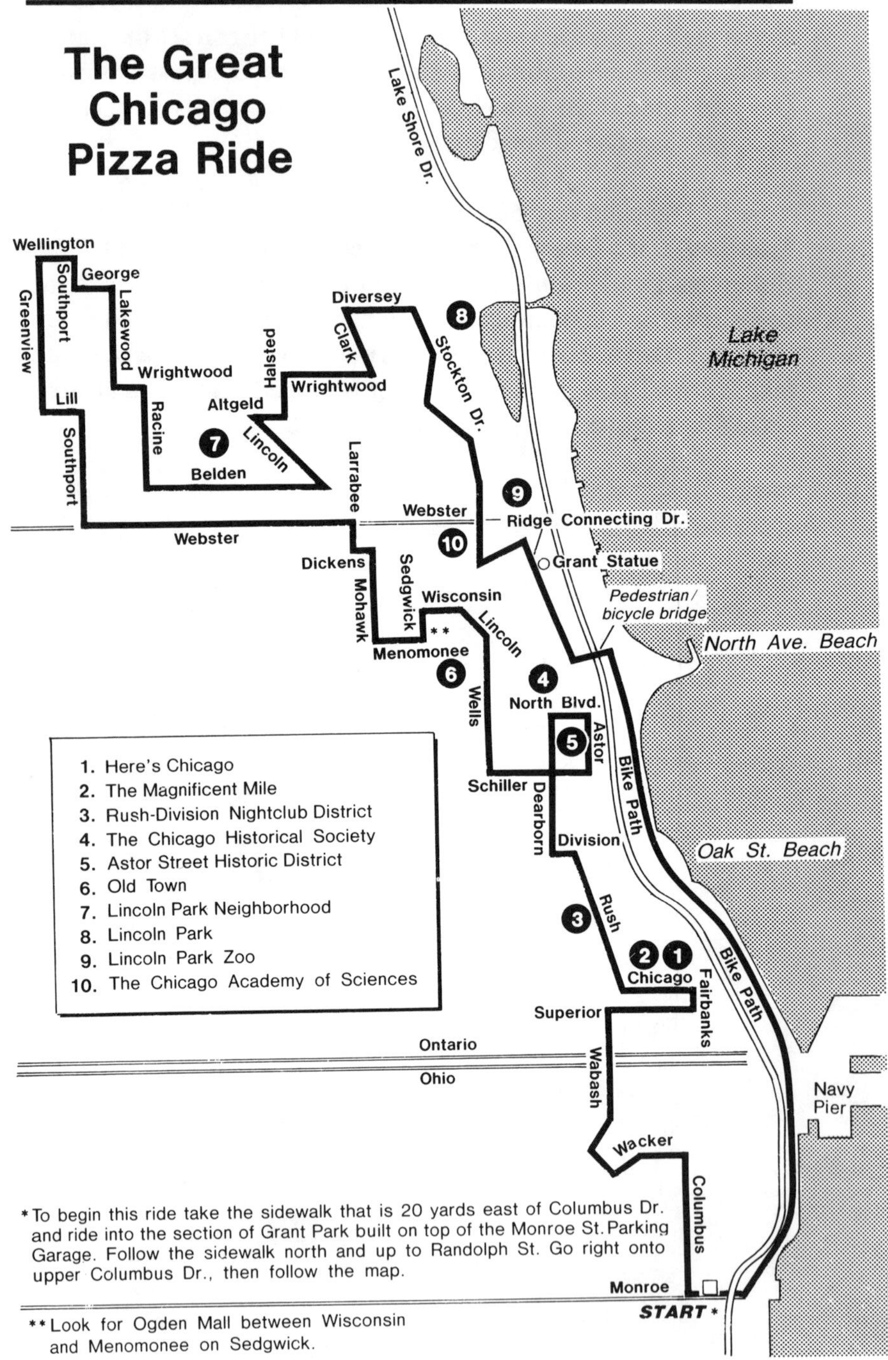
The Great Chicago Pizza Ride
Lake Shore Dr.
Lake Michigan
Wellington
George
Southport
Greenview
Lakewood
Diversey
Clark
Halsted
Wrightwood
Wrightwood
Altgeld
Racine
Lill
Southport
Lincoln
Belden
Stockton Dr.
Larrabee
Webster
Webster
Ridge Connecting Dr.
Grant Statue
Dickens
Mohawk
Sedgwick
Wisconsin
Lincoln
Pedestrian/ bicycle bridge
North Ave. Beach
Menomonee
Wells
North Blvd.
Astor
Bike Path
Schiller
Dearborn
Division
Oak St. Beach
Rush
Chicago
Fairbanks
Bike Path
Superior
Ontario
Ohio
Wabash
Navy Pier
Wacker
Columbus
Monroe
START *
1. Here's Chicago
2. The Magnificent Mile
3. Rush-Division Nightclub District
4. The Chicago Historical Society
5. Astor Street Historic District
6. Old Town
7. Lincoln Park Neighborhood
8. Lincoln Park
9. Lincoln Park Zoo
10. The Chicago Academy of Sciences
* To begin this ride take the sidewalk that is 20 yards east of Columbus Dr. and ride into the section of Grant Park built on top of the Monroe St. Parking Garage. Follow the sidewalk north and up to Randolph St. Go right onto upper Columbus Dr., then follow the map.
** Look for Ogden Mall between Wisconsin and Menomonee on Sedgwick.

The Great Chicago Pizza Ride

Start/End: Intersection of Columbus Drive and Monroe Drive

Distance: 16.1 miles (shortcut reduces ride to 13.9 miles)

Time: 2-4 hours depending on sight-seeing and other stops

Difficulty/Safety: Easy-to-moderate distance
Light-to-heavy traffic conditions

Shortcut: Skip Wrightwood and West Lakeview Loop and save 2.2 miles

Bicycle Shops:

Village Cycle Center
1337 N. Wells Street
(312) 751-2488

Cycle Smithy
2468½ N. Clark Street
(312) 281-0444

Quick Release Bike Shop
1170 W. Armitage Ave.
(312) 871-3110

Buckingham Bike Shop
3126 N. Broadway Ave.
(312) 975-0050

Activities/Highlights:

Here's Chicago (multimedia show)
Chicago Avenue and Michigan Avenue

The Magnificent Mile
Stores and landmarks along Michigan Avenue

Rush Street and Division Street Nightclub District

The Chicago Historical Society
Clark Street and North Avenue
(312) 642-4600

Astor Street Historic District

Old Town
Historic shopping and entertainment area along Wells Street

Neighborhood of Lincoln Park
- DePaul University
- McCormick Row House District

Lincoln Park
- Lincoln Park Conservatory
  Stockton Drive and Fullerton Parkway

- Lincoln Park Zoo
  Stockton Drive and Webster Drive

- The Chicago Academy of Sciences
  2001 N. Clark Street
  (just south of Lincoln Park Zoo
  (312) 871-2668

Pizzerias Along the Route

Pizzeria Uno
29 E. Ohio
(312) 321-1000

Pizzeria Due
619 N. Wabash
(312) 943-2400

Gino's East of Chicago
160 E. Superior
(312) 943-1124

Giordano's
1840 N. Clark
(312) 944-6100

Ranalli's
1925 N. Lincoln
(312) 642-4700

Bacino's
2204 N. Lincoln
(312) 472-7400

O'Fame Pizzeria and Cafe
750 W. Webster
(312) 929-5111

Edwardo's Natural Pizza
2120 N. Halsted
(312) 871-3400

Renaldi's
2827 N. Broadway
(312) 248-2445

Ranalli's Pizzeria - M. Palucki

Skyline from Lincoln Park - Dan Broten

The Great Chicago Pizza Ride

"Chicago and pizza are indelibly linked. Nowhere in America is pizza more revered; many Chicagoans, in fact, debate pizza with greater passion than politics or sports."

Douglas Perry, Lincoln Park Magazine, Winter 1991

"Chicago is the best pizza town bar none"

Frank Brusciane, Owner Renaldi's Pizza

The Great Chicago Pizza Ride offers many tantalizing delights: the glitzy shopping mecca along the "Magnificent Mile" of Michigan Avenue, people watching along the Rush Street nightclub district, the neighborhood of Old Town Triangle, lovely Victorian architecture, peaceful tree-lined streets in Sheffield Square, the campus of DePaul University, and the world class attractions of Chicago's largest Park - Lincoln Park. But the most delicious delights are the nine featured pizzerias that line the route, each serving its own brand of world famous "Chicago-Style" pizza.

Chicago's status as the pizza capital of the United States can be traced to the establishment of Pizzeria Uno in 1943. Restaurant owner Ike Sewell was the first to hit on the "deep-dish" concept now known the world over as "Chicago Style deep-dish pizza." "Deep-dish" pizza features tomatoes, choice of toppings, and lots of cheese on a bed of dough "so thick as to require a knife and fork to devour." This new culinary delight slowly caught on and, in 1955, Ike Sewell opened Pizzeria Due one block from Pizzeria Uno, and both restaurants have had long lines of fanatic pizza lovers ever since.

The ride begins at Columbus Drive and Monroe Drive. On the north side of Monroe Drive (20 yards east of Columbus Drive) is a pedestrian/bicycle sidewalk that leads northward. Take this sidewalk north and up a slight incline into the section of Grant Park built on top of the Monroe Drive parking garage. Continue on this sidewalk with the tennis courts on your left and the gardens on your right. Looking south is Lake Michigan, Buckingham Fountain, Soldier Field, and the museums. Up ahead is the Richard J. Daley Bicentennial Plaza and ice skating rink. Stay to the west of Bicentennial Plaza and take the sidewalk up a slight incline to Randolph Street. On the northwest corner of Randolph and Columbus is the Amoco Building, Chicago's second tallest skyscraper. Cross Randolph Street at the traffic light and continue north on the elevated portion of Columbus Drive to Wacker Drive and the Chicago River. The distance is one-half mile from the starting point to the river.

Cross Wacker Drive and go west traveling along the south bank of the Chicago River. (Refer to The West Side Story section of this guide for historic details about this stretch of the route.) Continue west on Wacker Drive crossing Michigan Avenue one block to Wabash Avenue and the Irv Kupcinet Bridge. Irv Kupcinet, gossip columnist for the Chicago Sun Times, has been a leading civic figure in Chicago for half a century and this bridge is named in his honor. Make a right turn, crossing the Chicago River and continue north on Wabash Avenue.

As you cross the river it may be humbling to remember that this entire section of Chicago was destroyed by the Chicago Fire of 1871. In fact, the fire engulfed four square miles of Chicago's central business district, killed hundreds of people, and left thousands homeless.

Continue north on Wabash Avenue a third of a mile to Pizzeria Uno on the southwest corner of Wabash Avenue and Ohio Street. Pizzeria Due is located one block further north on Wabash Avenue at Ontario Street. The Arabic-looking building on the west side of Wabash Avenue is the Medinah Temple. Three blocks north, at Wabash Avenue and Superior Street, is Holy Name Cathedral, the flagship church for Chicagoland's two million Roman Catholics.

At Superior Street make a right turn and proceed east across Michigan Avenue to Gino's East at 160 East Superior Street. Established in 1966, Gino's East serves an even deeper "deep-dish" pizza than Pizzeria Uno or Due. It's worth peeking inside this long-standing Chicago institution. While most restaurants strive to keep their decor fresh and current, Gino's East has the same graffiti carved tables as when it first opened in the turbulent 1960s - proof that it's the food that matters most. Leaving Gino's East, continue east on Superior Street to Fairbanks Court, make a left and take Fairbanks Court one block to Chicago Avenue. The large institutions in this area include the Rehabilitation Institute of Chicago and Northwestern University's Chicago Campus and Hospital. At Chicago Avenue make a left turn and go west to Michigan Avenue.

Chicago's "Magnificent Mile" runs north and south along Michigan Avenue from the river to Oak Street. This section near Chicago Avenue is the very heart of the "Magnificent Mile" and one of the most exciting places in the city. Just across Michigan Avenue on the west is the historic landmark Chicago Water Tower, one of the few structures left standing after the Chicago Fire. On your immediate right is the old pumping house for the Water Tower. The Here's Chicago multimedia show and tourist shop is located inside the old pumping house. One block north is Water Tower Place and the Ritz Carlton Hotel. The Atrium Shopping Mall inside Water Tower Place is quite beautiful and a great place to people watch. Just north of Water Tower Place is the John Hancock Center. Its 100 stories makes it the third tallest building in Chicago. Take a few minutes to walk your bicycle up and down Michigan Avenue where you will find many of the biggest names in retail.

Before the turn of the century this stretch was known as Pine Street. It housed breweries, shipyards, factories, and immigrant ghettos. Since the late 1960s, Michigan Avenue has supplanted State Street as Chicago's principal showpiece and shopping street.

Proceed west on Chicago Avenue across Michigan Avenue one block to the traffic light at Rush Street. Make a right and go north on Rush Street passing Loyola University's downtown campus, and Pippins, a popular Irish watering hole.

Pedaling north you enter the nightclub and bar district known as Rush Street. This area is the principal entertainment district for Chicago's conventioneers and tourists, as well as a gathering place for impromptu celebrations. After the Chicago Bears won the Super Bowl in 1986, and the Bulls won the NBA championship in 1991 and 1992, Rush and Division Streets were mobbed with thousands of celebrating Chicagoans. The total distance from the starting point to Rush Street and Division Street is 2.7 miles.

At Division Street make a left turn and pedal west, passing all of the singles bars, one block to Dearborn Street. At Dearborn Street, go right and pedal one-half mile to North Boulevard and the Chicago Historical Society. This general vicinity (including the Rush Street nightclub district) is known as the "Gold Coast," and is Chicago's most prestigious residential neighborhood. The Gold Coast extends from Lake Shore Drive on the east to LaSalle Street on the west, and from Oak Street on the south to North Boulevard on the north.

During the 1850s and 1860s, this area marked the northern limits of the city and north of North Avenue was an old cemetery which was converted to a city park. In 1865, shortly after the assassination of President Abraham Lincoln, the park was renamed Lincoln Park. Cross North Boulevard and enter Lincoln Park. The large building on the left, officially at North Avenue and Clark Street, is the Chicago Historical Society. On the east side of the museum, and not to be missed, is sculptor Augustus Saint-Gauden's masterpiece statue of Abraham Lincoln - The Standing Lincoln.

Proceed east on North Boulevard in the direction of Lake Michigan. On your right, at 1555 N. State Parkway, is a very large, red brick, Queen Anne style mansion with 19 chimneys. This home, designed in 1880, is the oldest house in the Gold Coast. Since 1885, it has been the residence for Chicago's Roman Catholic Archbishop. One block further east is Astor Street and the Astor Street Historic

District. Make a right on Astor Street and proceed south to Schiller Street. Astor Street, named after John Jacob Astor a pioneer fur trader, is considered the heart of the Gold Coast. Starting in the early 1880s and continuing into the 1890s, Chicago's wealthiest and most powerful citizens, attracted by the lakefront and proximity to downtown, began building mansions along Lake Michigan and Astor Street. The architectural styles favored by Chicago's elite included the Queen Anne style, Richardsonian Romanesque, and a mixture of Italian Renaissance, French Second Empire, English Georgian and American Colonial. To fully appreciate the architectural history of this area, contact the Chicago Architectural Foundation for guided tours.

The designated route takes you west on Schiller Street .6 mile to North Avenue and Wells Street in Old Town. (However, feel free to further explore Astor Street and State Parkway before returning to the route.) Continue west on Schiller crossing State Parkway, Dearborn Street, Clark Street, La Salle Street and finally arriving at Wells Street. Make a right on Wells Street and proceed north. (Watch out for car doors opening in traffic.) This stretch of Wells Street used to be the heart of Chicago's bohemian community with health food restaurants, folk music clubs, head shops and funky bars. If your interested, lock your bicycle and wander into any of the shops or restaurants. As you cross North Avenue, on the left is Second City, the world famous improvisational comedy theater that produced stars James and John Belushi.

Continue north on Wells Street about .3 mile to Giordano's Famous Stuffed Pizza on the northeast corner of Wells Street and Lincoln Avenue. The actual entrance for Giordano's is around the corner at 1840 N. Clark Street. Stuffed pizza features a blend of three cheeses and all fresh ingredients between two layers of crust. If you have never tasted stuffed pizza, then Giordano's is the place to try it.

Make a left on Lincoln Avenue and proceed .2 mile to Ranalli's Pizzeria, just north of the stop sign at Wisconsin Street. Many people rave about Ranalli's "thin crust" pizza, but the real highlight of this restaurant is its large and lively outdoor cafe. Next, the designated route takes you one mile from Ranalli's to Bacino's Pizzeria at Lincoln Avenue and Webster Avenue.

Leave Ranalli's by retracing your route a half block south to the stop sign at Wisconsin Street. Make a right turn and go west on Wisconsin two blocks to Sedgwick Street. Go left on Sedgwick and pedal a half block south looking for the entrance to a small park and pedestrian path on the west side of the street. **Walk** your bicycle up one of the driveways and slowly work your way west along the pedestrian path of Ogden Mall. The Ogden Mall serves as a pedestrian link between the western sections of this neighborhood, with Lincoln Park on the east. About midway along the Ogden Mall are Sculptor John Kearney's Two Horses. Completed in 1975, they are made from unused auto bumpers welded together in lifelike images. On the western end of the Ogden Mall and south of the fountain is the Midwest Buddhist Temple, serving Chicago's Buddhist population since 1971.

John Kearney's Two Horses - M. Palucki

Just south of Ogden Mall are the narrow streets of the old German neighborhood called Old Town Triangle. The designated route goes west on Menomonee Street, but take a few minutes to explore Hudson Avenue, St. Michaels Court, or Cleveland Avenue. In 1976, the Old Town Triangle was declared a Chicago Landmark District, thereby preserving the refurbished 1870 to 1890 Victorian frame cottages and Brownstones that line the quaint streets. Just south of the temple, at Eugenie Street and Cleveland Avenue, is St. Michaels Church, Chicago's oldest German Catholic Church founded in 1852.

Leave Old Town and the Old Town Triangle by pedaling westbound on Menomonee Street. Two blocks west of the Midwest Buddhist Temple is Mohawk Street where you make a right and travel north until it ends at Dickens Avenue. You are now in the neighborhood of Lincoln Park, whose official boundaries are Armitage Avenue on the south; Diversey Parkway on the north; Southport Avenue on the west; and Lake Shore Drive on the east. Lincoln Park followed the settlement patterns of Old Town with older German and Irish settlers giving way to Swedish, Romanian, African-American, and Hispanic newcomers. Today, Lincoln Park is the neighborhood of choice for Chicago's young professionals.

At Dickens Avenue go left one block west to Larrabee Street. Make a right at Larrabee Street and pedal one block to the traffic lights at Lincoln Avenue, Webster Avenue, and Larrabee Street. On your left is Oz Park, with its ball fields, tennis courts, playlot, and sight of numerous summer festivals. At 2204 N. Lincoln Avenue, just three store fronts north of Webster Avenue, is Bacino's Pizza. Carefully make a left onto westbound Webster Avenue and walk on the west sidewalk of Lincoln Avenue.

Bacino's is famous for its "Heart-Healthy" stuffed spinach pizza, which it claims meets the American Heart Association standards for fat and cholesterol. Only in Lincoln Park, with its surplus of health conscious young people, can you find this kind of a pizza place. The total distance from the starting point is 6.1 miles.

Continue west on Webster Avenue .2 mile to O'Fame Pizzeria and Cafe at Webster and Halsted. John Casale, owner of O'Fame, comes from a long-standing pizza making family. Mr. Casale takes exception with the praise and publicity of the corporate "Chicago Style" pizza chains and thinks the Uno's and Gino's of the city, "might be great for tourism but limits peoples pizza tastes and closes minds to family run pizzerias."

Just west of O'Fame is Halsted Street which has recently become a popular entertainment district. About one-half block south, at 2120 N. Halsted Street, is Edwardo's Natural Pizza. Edwardo's serves a popular and fine tasting stuffed pizza that has won its share of accolades.

Continue west on Webster Avenue .3 mile to Sheffield Avenue in the heart of Sheffield Square. Bounded by Halsted Street on the east; Fullerton Avenue on the north; Armitage Avenue on the south; and Racine Avenue on the west, Sheffield Square is closely associated with DePaul University which is just one block north of Webster Avenue. Along many of the north and south side streets are rehabilitated turn-of-the-century row houses. As you pass under the combined Howard and Ravenswood El tracks, you are in the heart of Sheffield Square. On the northwest corner of Sheffield Avenue and Webster Avenue is St. Vincent's Catholic Church established in 1897.

Next, its on to West Lakeview. Continue west on Webster Avenue .4 mile to Southport Avenue. During the 1920s, Webster Avenue, between Racine Avenue and Southport Avenue, was the center of Chicago's Romanian community. At 1339 W. Webster is the old Romanian Greek Orthodox Church that has now been converted into a private residence. Just west of Southport is Clybourn Avenue which until recently was an industrial and commercial zone. "Clybourn Corridor" (as it is now known), has emerged as a major shopping district, rivaling the established Lincoln Park retail district along Clark Street.

Wrightwood and West Lakeview Loop

The Wrightwood and West Lakeview Loop is a 2.2 mile trip through the old German neighborhood of West Lakeview. To bypass this loop, take Southport Avenue north one block and make a right onto Belden Avenue. Take Belden Avenue east and pickup the designated route four blocks east at Racine Avenue.

You will begin the Wrightwood and West Lakeview Loop by pedaling north on Southport past St. Josaphat's Catholic Church, founded in 1902 for Chicago's German speaking Polish community. Cross Fullerton Avenue and proceed two blocks to Lill Avenue. Take Lill Avenue left and go west one block to Wrightwood Playground on Greenview Avenue. Wrightwood is a small community of mainly frame two-flats, with a increasing number of new constructions. Continuing north on Greenview Avenue, at Wrightwood Avenue, is the exclusive Embassy Club residential housing development. Continue north on Greenview, crossing busy Diversey Parkway, all the way to Wellington Avenue. Make a right on Wellington and go east one block to Southport Avenue. On the southwest corner is Zum Deuchen Eck whose authentic decor and superb food makes it one of the best German restaurants in the city.

West Lakeview, while undergoing considerable renovation, continues to be a more traditional neighborhood with ethnic working-class and young professionals making up most of the population. Make a right and go south on Southport Avenue two blocks to George Street. Looking behind you on north Southport Avenue is the giant steeple of St. Alphonsus Church established in 1882. At George Street go left and travel east one block to Lakewood Avenue. Make a right and take Lakewood Avenue south across Diversey Parkway to Wrightwood Avenue. Lakewood Avenue offers a good example of the original and newer residential architecture that exists in West Lakeview. Go left on Wrightwood two blocks east to Racine Avenue. Make a right on Racine Avenue, traveling south across Fullerton Avenue to Belden Avenue. The total distance for the Wrightwood and West Lakeview Loop is 2.2 miles.

Traveling east on Belden Avenue you enter the DePaul section of Lincoln Park. DePaul University was founded in 1898 and began its operations in the original St. Vincent's Church building on Webster Avenue at Kenmore Avenue. On your right, between Kenmore and Sheffield, is Alumni Hall, old home of the DePaul Blue Demons basketball team. As you cross Sheffield Avenue and pass under the El tracks you enter the stately east campus of DePaul University. These magnificent buildings used to be part of the McCormick Theological Seminary and luckily survived the Great Chicago Fire. Just east of Dayton Street is a driveway leading north to the McCormick Row House District. Enter the parking area and pedal around private Chalmers Place, part of the now individually owned row homes built by the seminary between 1884 and 1889. These simplified Queen Anne style row homes exemplify 19th century residential architecture and neighborhood planning. Return to Belden Avenue and continue east carefully crossing Halsted Street two blocks to Lincoln Avenue.

Rush Street -M. Palucki

At Lincoln Avenue go left, pass Childrens Memorial Hospital on your right, and carefully cross the Fullerton Avenue, Halsted Street, and Lincoln Avenue intersection. Just past the traffic light is a interesting retail district featuring many excellent bookstores, bars, restaurants, and movie theaters. On your right is the famous Biograph theater, where on July 22, 1934, in the alley just south of the theater, public enemy number one, John Dillinger, was gunned down after being identified by the "Lady in Red."

Continue north on Lincoln Avenue making a right turn at Altgeld Street. Take Altgeld Street east until it ends at Halsted Street. Carefully cross Halsted Street and go left, continuing north to the traffic light at Wrightwood Avenue. Make a right on Wrightwood and pedal east until it ends at the traffic light on Clark Street. Go left and follow Clark Street north a short ways to Diversey Parkway. Be careful of car doors opening into traffic.

Clark Street, originally an old Indian trail leading all the way to Green Bay, Wisconsin, is the principal shopping street in Lincoln Park. As you head north on Clark Street you approach the thriving retail intersection of Clark, Diversey, and Broadway. Clark and Diversey, as this shopping area is often referred, became an important retail area after the building boom of the 1890s. Today, this area is known as New Town and attracts a much more diverse population than Lincoln Park.

Next, the route takes you just a short distance north of Diversey Parkway on Broadway Street to Renaldi's Pizza. Renaldi's Pizza, at 2827 N. Broadway, serves delicious New York style pizza by the slice. Original owner Frank Brusciane opened Renaldi's in 1973 and his pizza is delicious. Return south on Broadway back to Diversey Parkway.

Make a left off Broadway and pedal east on Diversey Parkway .2 mile to the traffic light at Sheridan Road, Lakeview Avenue, and Stockton Drive. On the southwest corner is the Elks National Memorial and Headquarters Building. This beautiful and elaborate memorial is unique and worth taking a few minutes to explore. Carefully cross Lakeview Avenue and take Stockton Drive south and into Lincoln Park.

Lincoln Park is Chicago's oldest large park and has over 1,200 acres of park land. It began in the early 1860s as a cemetery near North Avenue and has since been extended many miles north to Hollywood Avenue. At the turn of the century, Lincoln Park was Chicago's premier recreation attraction. Almost 100 years later, it remains Chicago's most popular park.

After crossing Lakeview Avenue go right on Stockton Drive (the street running parallel to Lakeview Avenue). On your left is the impressive Johann Wolfgang von Goethe Monument dating back to 1913. Also on your left is the Alexander Hamilton sculpture. Feel free to explore the grounds around the Hamilton sculpture, then continue south on Stockton Drive. On your left is the lovely Sunshine Playlot and just beyond is North Pond. Across North Pond, you'll find the Park Place Cafe, and behind the cafe is Prospect Hill, which, together with North Pond, were laid out in the late 1870s. The route continues south on Stockton Drive along the west side of North Pond. Just south of the playlot is a small flat monument plaque, more like a grave marker, it identifies this ridge as the location of the Lake Michigan shoreline 800 years ago, when the lake elevation was 20 feet higher.

At the traffic light cross Fullerton Parkway and continue south on Stockton Drive. On your left is the Lincoln Park Conservatory, which, since 1892, has housed permanent and seasonal floral exhibits. Continuing south are the Formal Gardens and the Bates Fountain. Just beyond the fountain is the main entrance for the Lincoln Park Zoo.

Built in 1868 and recently remodeled, Lincoln Park Zoo is one of Chicago's finest attractions. With its free admission policy it is certainly Chicago's best entertainment value. By all means lock your bicycle and wander around the landscaped grounds. You will leave the zoo south along Stockton Drive.

About .3 mile south of the zoo and on your right is the Chicago Academy of Sciences. Across the street from the Academy is Cafe Brauer. Recently remodeled to it's original 1908 splendor, Cafe Brauer is a combination snack stand and second floor banquet hall. If your interested, take a few minutes to explore Cafe Brauer and the shoreline of South Pond. Here you'll find a paddle boat rental pier, snack shop, and roller skate rental office. This area is not a bicycle route so **walk** your bicycle. Work your way up the slight incline to the pedestrian bridge that crosses over South Pond. Just west and south of the pedestrian bridge is the Farm-in-the-Zoo with a functioning dairy barn and farm animals.

South Pond in Lincoln Park - Dan Broten

The designated route takes you to Ridge Connecting Drive (between Cafe Brauer and the Farm-In-The Zoo). Make a left and follow the roadway, over the pedestrian bridge, to the east side of South Pond. Follow Ridge Connecting Drive as it bends southwards and uphill to the Ulysses S. Grant Memorial. Completed in 1891, General Grant and his horse stand over 18 feet high and command a beautiful view of Lake Michigan and Lincoln Park. So, you might ask, why isn't General Grant in Grant Park? The answer has to do with timing. When General Grant died and this memorial was completed, the future Grant Park was still a mud covered swamp so they placed his statue in Lincoln Park.

Continue south and down the moderate incline toward the ballfields and the pedestrian/bicycle bridge that cross Lake Shore Drive. The distance from Lincoln Park Zoo to the pedestrian bridge is just under one mile. **Walk** your bicycle across the bridge making a right and continuing south along the Lakefront Bicycle Path .1 mile to the North Avenue Beach. For details regarding this portion of the lakefront refer to The Northside-Wrigleyville Ride. For most cyclists, these final miles southbound along the Lakefront Bicycle Path are quite familiar and on weekends very crowded. The route takes you south of North Avenue Beach .8 mile to Oak Street Beach, one mile to Grand Avenue, and finally one mile to the starting point at Monroe Drive and Columbus Drive. Total distance from Lincoln Park Zoo to the starting point is just under four miles.

Dan Broten

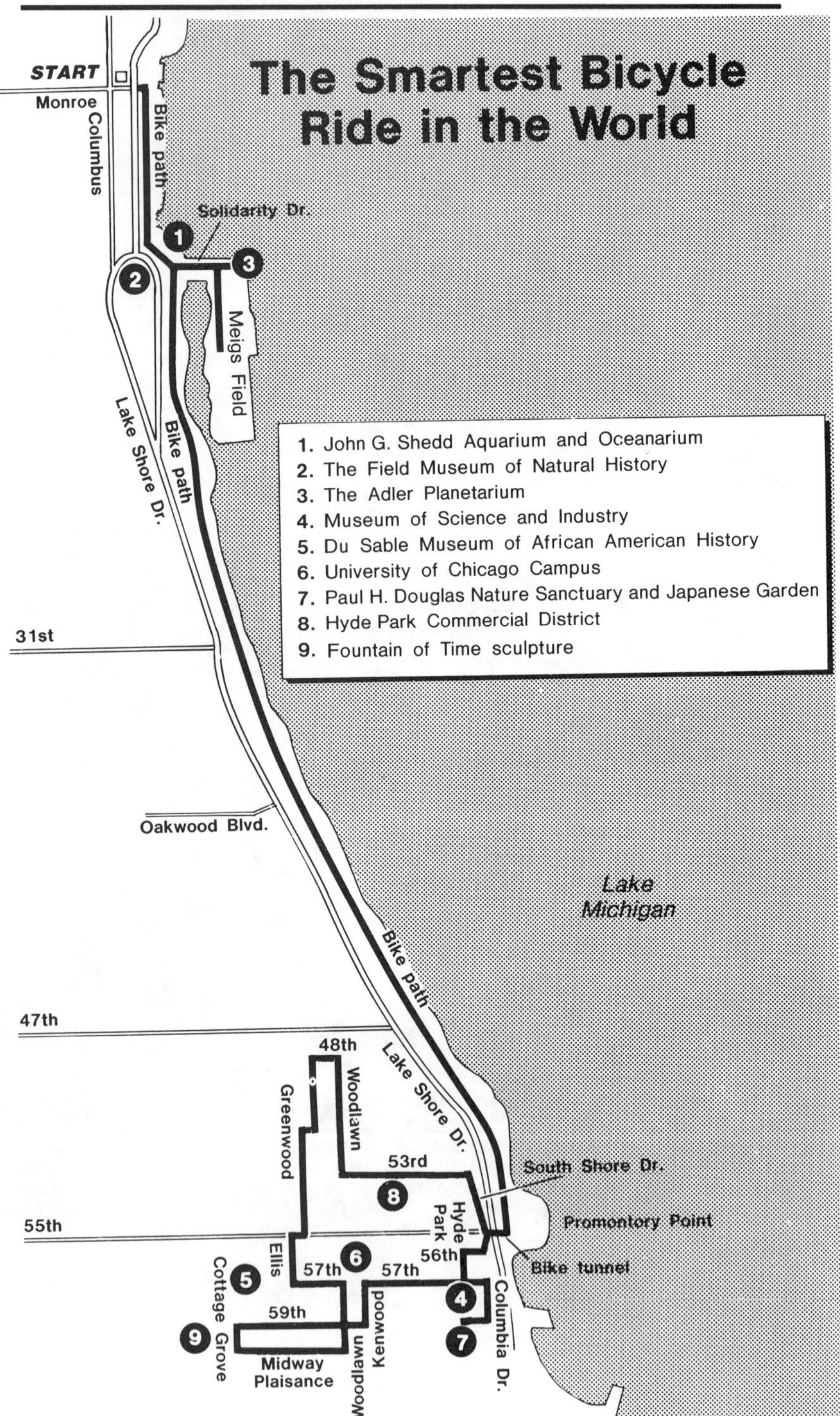
The Smartest Bicycle Ride in the World
START
Monroe
Columbus
Bike path
Solidarity Dr.
Meigs Field
Lake Shore Dr.
Bike path
1. John G. Shedd Aquarium and Oceanarium
2. The Field Museum of Natural History
3. The Adler Planetarium
4. Museum of Science and Industry
5. Du Sable Museum of African American History
6. University of Chicago Campus
7. Paul H. Douglas Nature Sanctuary and Japanese Garden
8. Hyde Park Commercial District
9. Fountain of Time sculpture
31st
Oakwood Blvd.
Lake Michigan
Bike path
47th
48th
Greenwood
Woodlawn
Lake Shore Dr.
53rd
South Shore Dr.
Hyde Park
Promontory Point
55th
Ellis
56th
Bike tunnel
Cottage Grove
57th
57th
59th
Kenwood
Columbia Dr.
Midway Plaisance
Woodlawn

The Smartest Bicycle Ride in the World

Start/End: Intersection of Columbus Drive and Monroe Drive

Distance: 23.6 miles (shortcuts reduce ride to as little as 6.5 miles)

Time: 2-5 hours depending on sight-seeing and other stops

Difficulty/Safety: Easy-to-strenuous distance
Light traffic conditions

Shortcuts:

1. Park at the Museum of Science and Industry and skip Lakefront Bicycle Path. New trip total 7.9 miles.
2. Skip Solidarity Drive Loop and save 1.8 miles.
3. Skip Wooded Island and Japanese Garden Loop and save 1.4 miles.

Bicycle Shops:

Turin Bicycle
435 E. Illinois Street
(312) 923-0100

Art's Cycle
1636 E. 55th Street
(312) 363-7524

Activities/Highlights:

John G. Shedd Aquarium and Oceanarium
1200 S. Lake Shore Drive
(312) 939-2426

The Field Museum of Natural History
1200 S. Lake Shore Drive
(312) 922-9410

The Adler Planetarium
1300 S. Lake Shore Drive
(312) 322-0300

Museum of Science and Industry
57th Street and Lake Shore Drive
(312) 684-1414

Du Sable Museum of African American History
740 E. 56th Place
(312) 947-0600

Chicago Architectural Foundation
Tours of Hyde Park, Kenwood, University of Chicago Campus and Frank Lloyd Wright's Robie House.
(312) 782-1776

Paul H. Douglas Nature Sanctuary and Japanese Garden on the Wooded Island in Jackson Park.

Hyde Park's commercial district along 53rd street

Jackson Park - M. Palucki

Japanese Garden - M. Palucki

Museum of Science and Industry - M. Palucki

Quadrangle at University of Chicago - M. Palucki

The Smartest Bicycle Ride in the World

"Fifty-seven Nobel Prize Winners have been associated with the University of Chicago as students or faculty."
University of Chicago Letter of Introduction

Carl Sagan - David Rockefeller - John Paul Stevens
Susan Sontag - Katharine Meyer Graham - Ed Asner
Milton Friedman - Kurt Vonnegut, Jr. - Studs Terkel
Charles Percy - Andrew Greeley - Mike Nichols -
Willie Davis - Saul Bellow
Notable University Of Chicago Alumni

The Smartest Bicycle Ride in the World provides all the elements for an enjoyable urban cycling adventure: miles of unobstructed lakefront riding, quiet tree-lined streets, colorful shopping districts with a wide diversity of ethnic restaurants, large mansions once owned by celebrities, several Frank Lloyd Wright masterpieces, the University of Chicago and its English collegiate Gothic style architecture, world class museums, significant public statuary, public parks designed by the world's foremost landscape architects, and an authentic Japanese garden. This route will take you along the Lakefront Bicycle Path and through the neighborhoods of Hyde Park and South Kenwood.

The ride begins at Columbus Drive and Monroe Drive. Travel east on the north sidewalk of Monroe Drive and cross Lake Shore Drive at the traffic light. Make a right on the Lakefront Bicycle Path and continue south through the heart of Grant Park. Travel 1.1 miles to Solidarity Drive and the John G. Shedd Aquarium and Oceanarium.

As you pedal south along the Lakefront Bicycle Path, you can see the sailboats rocking gently in Monroe Harbor, and, if it's windy, feel the mist off of Buckingham Fountain. Over your right shoulder is Chicago's magnificent skyline and directly in front of you, like an ancient Grecian ruin, is the Field Museum of Natural History. Designed, in part, by Daniel H. Burnham and funded by retail magnet Marshall Field, the Field Museum is modeled after the Erechteum on the Acropolis in Athens.

This section of Grant Park originally was a muddy shoreline and did not become a park until after the Chicago Fire of 1871. Using debris leftover from the fire the shoreline was filled in and, slowly, the distinct rectangular layout of the park came into existence. In 1901, the park was officially named Grant Park in honor of Civil War General and 18th President Ulysses S. Grant.

Visionary architect Daniel H. Burnham is perhaps the man most responsible for Chicago's lovely park-lined lakefront. In 1909, Burnham presented his Plan of Chicago, a plan that envisioned a lakefront of park land with formal gardens, cultural institutions and a place free from commercial exploitation. As a lasting tribute to Burnham's foresight and wisdom, Grant Park, today, is considered, "the largest, oldest, and architecturally most impressive cultural center in the United States." Making up this impressive cultural center are: The Fine Arts Building (1886), The Auditorium Theatre (1889), The Art Institute of Chicago (1894), Orchestra Hall (1904), The Field Museum of Natural History (1920), Clarence Buckingham Fountain (1926), Soldier Field (1926), The John G. Shedd Aquarium (1930), The Adler Planetarium (1930), The James C. Petrillo Music Shell, and countless public statuary.

Daniel H. Burnham was truly a towering figure in Chicago's development, and his famous quote is the unofficial motto for the City of Chicago.

> "...Make no little plans, they have no magic to stir men's blood and probably themselves will not be realized. Make big plans; aim high in hope and work..."

At the southern end of Monroe Harbor, facing Lake Michigan, is the John G. Shedd Aquarium. Named for its founder, a former president of Marshall Field and Company, it was modeled after classical Greek architecture and opened in 1930. The Oceanarium exhibit, opened in 1991, more than doubled the size of this cultural landmark, and now Chicagoans have a rare chance to see whales, dolphins, and other large ocean animals.

Burnham Park Yacht Harbor - M. Palucki

Solidarity Drive Loop

The designated route follows Solidarity Drive, which is just south of the Shedd Aquarium, east to Meigs Field and the Adler Planetarium. To shortcut the Solidarity Drive Loop, continue south on the Lakefront Bicycle Path and save 1.8 miles. Pedal eastbound on Solidarity Drive watching out for the parked cars and pedestrians as you make a 1.8-mile loop returning to the Aquarium. Named in honor of Poland's Solidarity Labor Union and its leader Lech Walesa, Solidarity Drive also confirms the importance of Chicago's Polish population - the largest concentration of Poles in the world outside of Warsaw, Poland. On your left is the statue of Thaddeus Kosciuszko, a Polish military engineer, who built the fortifications for Saratoga and West Point during the American Revolution. Just west of the Planetarium entrance is a statue of Polish astronomer Nicolaus Copernicus the father of modern astronomy.

Just before reaching the Planetarium take a right turn and follow the roadway south towards Meigs Field. On your right is Burnham Park Yacht Harbor with Soldier Field in the background. Looking north is another fantastic view of Chicago's skyline. Continue south until you reach the Meigs Field passenger terminal. Meigs Field, built on land created for the 1933 World's Fair, is used primarily by corporate jets.

Leave the airport by heading north, passing 12th Street Beach and arriving at the Adler Planetarium. Max Adler, a Sears, Roebuck executive, donated the money to build the Adler Planetarium and it is considered one the most beautiful structures in Chicago. The building is quite small on the surface, but, interestingly, most of the exhibits and observation areas are below ground level and the museum is actually much larger than it appears. As you circle the Planetarium, you can enjoy yet another wonderful view of Chicago's skyline. Continue west on Solidarity Drive and link up with the Lakefront Bicycle Path just south of the Shedd Aquarium.

Make a left and go south on the bicycle path one mile to

McCormick Place. Chicago owes its reputation as "convention center of the world" to McCormick Place and its almost 2 million square feet of exhibition space.

The route then takes you south along the Lakefront Bicycle Path 4.7 miles to Promontory Point and Hyde Park. For safety reasons, it is recommended that you remain on the bicycle path and not go west of Lake Shore Drive. This section of the Lakefront Bicycle Path is usually not crowded and winds through grassy park land with the choppy blue-green waters of Lake Michigan just a short distance away. If you're looking to ride hard and fast, then this is the stretch to go for it. As you ride south you may notice the shoreline is made up of rocky boulders and chunks of concrete. As expressways and other construction projects were initiated, much of the debris was hauled to the lakefront and used to fill the shoreline outward into Lake Michigan. No other city in America has been so successful at preserving greenways along its shoreline, and, today, Chicago has 18 miles of lakefront parks stretching along Lake Michigan.

Riding south, you pass 31st Street Beach and just beyond is the pedestrian bridge at 35th Street. Looking west, on the other side of the pedestrian bridge, you can see the statue of Stephen A. Douglas atop the 100-foot pillar marking his tomb. Douglas was a powerful United States Senator during the decade preceding the American Civil War. He used his influence to get the Illinois Central Railroad (IC) rights to build a rail line along Lake Michigan. The Illinois Central railroad tracks are just west of Lake Shore Drive and continue to carry thousands of commuters into Chicago daily. Continue south on the bicycle path to 47th Street to the best photo point on the South Side for Chicago's skyline.

Continue south to Promontory Point at 55th Street. At Promontory Point follow the path to the left and **walk** your bicycle to the point. This scenic spot is a great place to picnic and rest before continuing on your route. To the north is the Chicago skyline and to the south, the Museum of Science and Industry, the Henry Crown Space Center, 57th Street Beach, and Jackson Park. Circle around

Promontory Point and **walk** your bicycle under Lake Shore Drive through the 55th Street pedestrian/bicycle tunnel.

Emerging from the 55th Street pedestrian tunnel you encounter a row of affluent high rise condominiums stretching along a greenway in front of Lake Shore Drive. You have entered the neighborhood of Hyde Park and will bicycle 7.9 miles through Hyde Park and South Kenwood returning to this same pedestrian tunnel.

In 1853, a young attorney named Paul Cornell, taking the advise of Senator Stephen A. Douglas, purchased 300 acres of land along Lake Michigan between 51st Street and 55th Street. Cornell's dream was to build a upper-middle class suburb free from factories and commercial activities. His suburb, named Hyde Park, was to evoke the stately elegance of like-named communities in London and New York. In 1889, the City of Chicago annexed Hyde Park and three years later, in 1892, the University of Chicago opened its campus in Hyde Park. One year later, in 1893, Chicago's Hyde Park hosted the World's Columbian Exposition - a world's fair honoring Columbus's discovery of the new world 400 years earlier. Today, Hyde Park and South Kenwood are an island within Chicago's inner city south side. Both physically, through a series of parks and boulevards, and intellectually, with thousands of the nation's brightest students and faculty members, Hyde Park and South Kenwood are a world apart from its poorer surroundings.

Continue west on the sidewalk after emerging from the 55th Street tunnel. When the sidewalk ends at South Shore Drive go right and follow the Drive north as it zigzags to 53rd Street. At 5300 South Shore Drive is the Hampton House where now deceased Mayor Harold Washington resided while Mayor of Chicago. Go left on 53rd Street and continue west under the Illinois Central Railroad tracks and into Hyde Park's principal commercial district. Along this flourishing shopping street are a wide selection of restaurants and stores that reflect the diversity of Hyde Park. American fast-food, Middle Eastern, Thai, Chinese, Sushi, Health Food, and Barbecue Ribs can all be found along this short stretch of roadway. Neighborhood grocery stores and discount shops share the street with hightech computer centers and highbrow bookstores.

Continue west on 53rd Street and make a right turn onto Woodlawn Avenue. At 5132 Woodlawn Avenue is Frank Lloyd Wright's 1897 Heller House. Take Woodlawn Avenue past Hyde Park Boulevard and enter the South Kenwood neighborhood. Kenwood, founded by Dr. John Kennicott and named after his mother's hometown in Scotland, developed into one of Chicago's premier neighborhoods. At one time Chicago's biggest names in meat packing, steel, and real estate built their twenty room mansions on Kenwood Avenue, Ellis Avenue, and Woodlawn Avenue between 48th Street and Hyde Park Boulevard.

Feel free to wander off the designated route, though it's recommended that you do not go north of 48th Street or west of Ellis Avenue. Notable buildings in the area include the former home of Muhammad Ali (located two houses north of 50th Street on the west side of Woodlawn Avenue), and on the northeast corner of 49th Street and Woodlawn Avenue is the home of late Black Muslim leader Elijah Muhammad. Kenwood's close proximity to the Union Stockyards along with its convenient access to downtown Chicago led to its rise as an affluent suburb. During its heyday, in the mid and late 1800s, Kenwood was known as the "Lake Forest of the South Side." However, Kenwood's proximity to public transportation, along with the growth and aroma of the Stockyards, also spelled its doom. As working class people began moving into Kenwood the wealthy moved on to other neighborhoods.

Get back on the designated route at 48th Street and Woodlawn Avenue. Go west one block on 48th Street and go left on Greenwood Avenue. Continue south on Greenwood Avenue all the way to 55th Street, watching for the slight jog to the right at Hyde Park Boulevard.

At 55th Street go right one block to Ellis Avenue and make a left turn. As you cross 55th Street on Ellis Avenue, you will enter the campus of the University of Chicago. The University of Chicago, founded by John D. Rockefeller of the Standard Oil Company, celebrated its centennial on October 1, 1992. The University's original architect, Henry Ives Cobb, designed the campus around a series of formal quadrangles. Using gray Indiana limestone and an English collegiate Gothic style, the campus resembles a medieval walled city. The setting is quite impressive and all together fitting for one of the most prestigious and, incidently, most expensive universities in the world. Announcements of new discoveries and profound truths are routine in Hyde Park; a place where more Nobel Prize winners live than anywhere else on earth.

The Universisty of Chicago and Midway Plaisance - M. Palucki

Just south of 56th Street on the east side of Ellis Avenue is Henry Moore's famous sculpture "Nuclear Energy." Completed in 1967, "Nuclear Energy" commemorates the site of the University of Chicago's world-changing accomplishment - the earth's first self-sustaining controlled nuclear reaction. On December 2, 1942, under the Stagg Field grandstands, scientists led by Italian Physicist Enrico Fermi propelled the world into the atomic age, cumulating with the dropping of the atomic bomb on Hiroshima August 6, 1945.

Make a left turn onto eastbound 57th Street and travel one-half block and look for a formal entrance gate on your right. Pass through the gate and enter the main quadrangle of the University of Chicago. Take a few minutes to pedal through the quadrangle returning the same way back to east 57th Street. Continue east on 57th past University Avenue to Woodlawn Avenue. The stately First Unitarian Church and its beautiful towering steeple is on the corner of 57th Street and Woodlawn Avenue. Go right on Woodlawn Avenue and travel south one block to 58th Street. On the northeast corner, at 5757 S. Woodlawn Avenue, stands Frank Lloyd Wright's masterpiece Robie House. Designed in 1906, it is considered to be "one of the most significant buildings in in the history of architecture." The Chicago Architectural Foundation can arrange tours of the Robie House. One block south on Woodlawn Avenue at 59th Street and rising to over 200 feet is the modern Gothically designed Rockefeller Chapel. This non-denominational church is perhaps the most striking object in all of Hyde Park and well worth a look inside.

Just south of 59th Street is Midway Plaisance. Midway Plaisance was so-named by landscape architect Frederick Law Olmsted whose original conceptual plans called for a greenway and water filled canal to be the midway connecting link with the lagoons and ponds of Jackson Park and Washington Park. Unfortunately there was never enough money to construct a connecting waterway and the city had to settle for the parklike "Midway." The name took on a whole new meaning as a result of the 1893 World's Columbian Exposition. The Exposition was held throughout Jackson Park, and along Midway Plaisance were the carnival rides and other attractions of the "Midway." The Midway was "the place to be in 1893," since that time, every county or state fair in the United States has had its own "Midway."

The route takes you right on 59th Street where you travel parallel to Midway Plaisance to the western end at Cottage Grove Avenue. Carefully cross Cottage Grove Avenue and just south near the entrance to Washington Park is one of Chicago's most unique and acclaimed pieces of public sculpture. Sculptor Lorado Taft's Fountain of Time took 14 years to create and was finally dedicated in 1922. Ira Bach's, Guide to Chicago's Public Sculpture states that themes of birth, struggle for existence, love, family life, religion, poetry, and war are all depicted by the "waves" of humanity moving across the landscape of time.

For those interested, the Du Sable Museum of African American History is located just south of the Fountain of Time at 740 E. 56th Place. Leave the Fountain of Time by taking Midway Plaisance east .7 mile to Woodlawn Avenue. Go left on Woodlawn Avenue a short distance to 59th Street. Make a right onto eastbound 59th Street and go two blocks to Kenwood Avenue. Make a left at Kenwood, crossing the cul-de-sac and passing University High School. Take Kenwood Avenue two blocks north to 57th Street. 57th Street is a small shopping district serving the University of Chicago.

Go right on eastbound 57th Street passing under the Illinois Central Railroad tracks and then carefully cross Stony Island Avenue and Cornell Drive. As you enter the Museum of Science and Industry parking lot you are on Museum Drive. Veer to your right and head for the main entrance. The present Museum of Science and Industry began as the Palace of Fine Arts for the 1893 Columbian Exposition. That original building was destroyed; the present building is an upgraded replica. The Museum of Science and Industry is considered to be one of the foremost museums in the world and has an incredible collection of "hands-on" exhibits. It would be unusual to find a Chicagoan who did not spend at least one day of their youth on a grammar school field trip to the museum.

Baseball and Bicycles - Dan Broten

Japanese Garden Loop

The final Hyde Park leg is to the Japanese Garden on the Wooded Island in Jackson Park. Take Museum Drive east along the front of the museum. At the eastern end of the museum is Columbia Drive. Follow it right, making your way past the Henry Crown Space Center and Omni Max Theater, past the railroad car exhibits and into Jackson Park. Once inside Jackson Park follow the pedestrian/bicycle path to the right and around the back of the museum. Continue following this path until you come to a small pedestrian/bicycle bridge with the Columbia Basin (Reflecting Pool) between you and the Museum of Science and Industry. This bridge, known as the Clarence Darrow Bridge, honors the attorney who won the 1925 Scopes Monkey Trial. Darrow, a long time Hyde Parker, so enjoyed this particular spot that he requested his ashes be scattered from this bridge. From this vantage point, it's easy to see how Darrow could fall in love with the beauty and peacefulness of Jackson Park.

Jackson Park was originally part of the South Parks. The South Parks Commission hired Frederick Law Olmsted and Calvert Vaux, who had both laid out New York's Central Park, to oversee the planning and design of the South Parks. In 1871, they presented their plans for water-oriented Jackson Park. Over the years many of Olmsted and Vaux's design concepts were realized and today Jackson Park is arguably Chicago's most beautiful park.

Continue west across the Clarence Darrow bridge and veer to the left looking for the narrow pedestrian/bicycle bridge to the Wooded Island. The Wooded Island, now officially known as the Paul H. Douglas Nature Sanctuary, was one of the Jackson Park's original design features. Hundreds of different bird species have been identified on the island and bird watching tours can be arranged through the Chicago Audubon Society. The authentic Japanese Garden, located on the north end of the Wooded Island (on your left as you cross the bridge), was first constructed in 1893 for the World's Columbian Exposition. Remodeled in 1981 the Japanese Garden provides a tranquil setting for meditation and contemplation.

Lock your bicycle at the garden entrance and follow the marked path.

After leaving the Japanese Garden take some time to further explore Jackson Park, but use caution as this is a large urban park. For those returning on the designated route, retrace your path back to the Museum of Science and Industry.

Exit the museum parking lot by crossing 57th Drive at the traffic light and proceed north on Hyde Park Boulevard to 56th Street. Go right and continue east on 56th Street until it ends at South Shore Drive. Go left and take South Shore Drive north to 55th Street and the pedestrian/bicycle tunnel under Lake Shore Drive. **Walk** your bicycle under Lake Shore Drive and take the Lakefront Bicycle Path left and north..

From the Museum of Science and Industry to Solidarity Drive and the Shedd Aquarium is 6 miles. Continue north on the Lakefront Bicycle Path 1.2 miles to the starting point at Monroe Drive and Columbus Drive.

The West Side Story

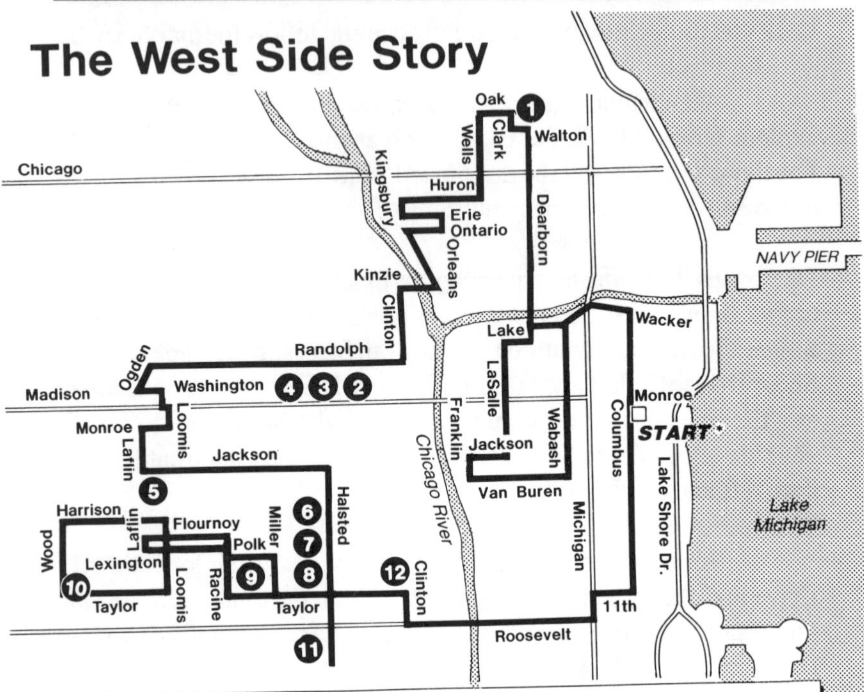

1. The Newberry Library
2. Randolph Street Market
3. Oprah Winfrey Studios
4. Museum of Holography
5. Jackson Boulevard Historic District
6. Greektown
7. Jane Addams Hull House Museum
8. University of Illinois
9. Little Italy
10. West Side Medical Center
11. Maxwell Street Market
12. Chicago Fire Department Academy

* To begin this ride take the sidewalk that is 20 yards east of Columbus Drive and ride into the section of Grant Park built on top of the Monroe Street Parking Garage. Follow the sidewalk north and up to Randolph Street. Go right onto *upper* Columbus Drive, then follow the map.

The West Side Story

Start/End: Intersection of Columbus Drive and Monroe Drive

Distance: 14.8 miles (shortcuts reduce ride to 10.6 miles and optional sidetrips increase ride to 17.5 miles)

Time: 2 to 3 hours depending on sight-seeing and other stops

Difficulty/Safety: Easy-to-moderate distance
Moderate traffic

Shortcuts:

1. Skip Union Park/Jackson Boulevard Historic District Loop and save 2.5 miles.
2. Skip West Side Medical Center Loop and save 1 mile.
3. Skip Maxwell Street Market Loop and save .7 mile.

Optional Sidetrips:

1. The "Loop" Loop - 2.2 miles.
2. Campus of University of Illinois at Chicago - .5 mile.

Bicycle Shops:

Village Cycle Center	Mt. Chicago	Irv's Bike Shop
1337 N. Wells	728 W. Randolph	1725 S. Racine
(312) 751-2488	(312) 685-5688	(312) 226-6330

Activities/Highlights:

The Newberry Library
60 West Walton
(312) 943-9090

Randolph Street Market
Randolph and Halsted Streets.

Harpo Studios, Inc. and The Oprah Winfrey Show
1058 West Washington Blvd.

Museum of Holography
1134 West Washington Blvd.
(312) 226-1007

Jackson Boulevard Historic District

Greektown
Halsted Street between Adams Street and Van Buren Street

Jane Addams Hull-House Museum
800 South Halsted
(312) 413-5353

Campus of the University of Illinois at Chicago
Entrance at Jane Addams Hull-House Museum

Little Italy
Taylor Street between Halsted and Ashland

West Side Medical Center

Maxwell Street Market
Maxwell Street and Halsted Street

Chicago Fire Department Fire Academy and "The Flame"
Taylor Street and Jefferson Street

Arrigo Park in Little Italy - Dan Broten

The Chicago River - Dan Broten

The West Side Story

"Genius is but audacity and the audacity of Chicago has chosen a star. It has worked upward to it and knows nothing that it fears to attempt and thus far has found nothing it can't accomplish."

Chicago Mayor Carter H. Harrison
October 28, 1893

"...it was the immigrants and not the Lake Shore residents who made Chicago and still keep it running. Without them, Chicago would not be"

Andrew M. Greeley, Chicago Tribune Magazine
May 23, 1976

The West Side Story is the story of Chicago's evolution from its industrial and immigrant origins to todays middle class service oriented neighborhoods. This ride will take you through Chicago's central business district, the restaurant and art gallery district of River North, the rapidly changing commercial district on the Near West Side, Greektown, the campus of the University of Illinois at Chicago, Little Italy, the West Side Medical Center, the Maxwell Street Market, and finally the site where the Great Chicago Fire of 1871 started. Although the immigrants are mostly gone, their neighborhoods still retain at least some resemblance to their colorful past.

Chicago's emergence as one of the great cities of the late 19th century was accomplished with the blood and sweat of its immigrant citizens. Between 1850 and the end of World War I, almost one million immigrants came to live and work in Chicago. In the city's relatively brief history it has been, "either the largest or second-largest Polish, Lithuanian, Jewish, Swedish, and Irish city in the world."

The ride begins at Columbus Drive and Monroe Drive. On the north side of Monroe Drive and 20 yards east of Columbus Drive is a pedestrian/bicycle sidewalk that leads northward. Take this sidewalk north and up a slight incline into the section of Grant Park built on top of the Monroe Drive parking garage. Continue on this sidewalk with the tennis courts on your left and the gardens on your right. Ahead is the Richard J. Daley Bicentennial Plaza and ice skating rink. Stay west of Bicentennial Plaza and take the sidewalk up a slight incline to Randolph Street. Cross Randolph Street at the traffic light and continue north on the elevated portion of Columbus Drive to Wacker Drive and the Chicago River. The distance is one-half mile from the starting point to the Chicago River.

Cross Wacker Drive and go west pedaling along the north side of Wacker Drive with the Chicago River on your right. In 1673, French explorers Father Jacques Marquette and Louis Jolliet paddled up this same, albeit slightly less "concretized," stretch of river. The local Indians called this area Checagou, which meant "wild onion" or "skunk," and for the next 200 years, industrial Chicago would do its best to live up to its name.

In 1837, when Chicago was incorporated as a city, there were over 4,000 people living in this vicinity. Most of Chicago's early development was along the same stretch of river that you are now riding. Wharves, warehouses, lumber yards, factories, and and other commercial operations were strung along the river banks. In 1847, on the north side of the river and just east of Michigan Avenue, Cyrus Hall McCormick built his grain reaper machine manufacturing plant. His machines, which would one day become world famous under the International Harvester name, were able to cut and bail two acres of grain per hour which revolutionized American farming.

As you approach Michigan Avenue all reference to Chicago's

humble past is lost in the shadows cast by the beautiful skyscrapers that hug the once wild shoreline. Looking east and west along the river are the marvelous architectural achievements of modern man: The Wrigley Building, The Tribune Tower, the cylindrical Marina Towers, further west the Merchandise Mart one of the largest wholesale buyers complex in the world, and down the river just out of sight, the world's tallest building, the Sears Tower. Continue west along Wacker Drive crossing Michigan Avenue and proceeding to Wabash Avenue. It may be easier to walk along the north sidewalk thereby avoiding the heavy traffic on Wacker Drive. To continue on the designated route, proceed west on Wacker Drive to Dearborn Street.

"Loop" Loop

Wacker Drive at Wabash Avenue is just north of Chicago's "Loop." The "Loop," named for the early streetcars that circled the downtown area, is now encircled by the famous iron elevated "El" lines. This section has been Chicago's central business district since its earliest days and was completely destroyed by the Great Chicago Fire.

The optional "Loop" Loop is 2.2 miles and returns to the Dearborn Street bridge. Chicago's "Loop" is a busy and bustling place and, therefore, it is recommended for only **experienced** cyclists. Take Wabash Avenue south under the famous "Loop" elevated "El" line to Van Buren Street. Make a right at Van Buren Street and continue west to Franklin Street. Go right on Franklin Street, then go north one block to Jackson Boulevard. On the northwest corner of Jackson and Franklin is the 110-story Sears Tower. Take Jackson Boulevard right and go east one block to LaSalle Street.

At LaSalle Street make a left and go north all the way to the elevated tracks over Lake Street. La Salle Street is Chicago's legal, financial, banking, and political center, with the Chicago Board of Trade anchoring the southern end of LaSalle Street at Jackson

Boulevard. City Hall is at Washington Boulevard with the mayor's office on the 5th floor. The "Loop" is a living museum of urban architecture and tours can be arranged through the Chicago Architectural Foundation. Take Lake Street right and go east two blocks to Dearborn Street. Take Dearborn left and proceed north crossing the Chicago River and continue along the designated route.

Picasso Sculpture in Richard J. Daley Plaza - Dan Broten

The designated route takes you across the Dearborn Street bridge and northward .9 mile to Washington Square Park. North of the river is Kinzie Street now also known as Haray Caray Drive. Haray Caray, longtime baseball voice for the Chicago Cubs, is one of Chicago's most beloved citizens. Further north at Dearborn Street and Ontario Street is the Excalibur nightclub. Until 1932, the Chicago Historical Society occupied this same 19th century building which was designed by Henry Ives Cobb, the same architect who designed the University of Chicago. Ontario Street has become one of Chicago's most visited restaurant and nightclub districts and within a short walk is the Hard Rock Cafe, Ed Debeviks, Walter Payton's America's Bar, and Pizzeria Uno and Due.

Continue north on Dearborn Street to Washington Square Park at Walton Street. The park, known to locals as "Bughouse Square," is one of the oldest parks in the city dating back to 1842. This neighborhood, for much of the late 1800s, was home to many of Chicago's wealthiest citizens and scattered throughout the area are old mansions and townhomes. Just north of Washington Square on Walton Street between Dearborn Street and Clark Street is one of the nation's foremost research libraries - the Newberry Library.

Leaving Washington Square you travel .6 mile to the heart of River North at Huron Street and Wells Street. Take Walton Street to Clark Street and go right to Oak Street. Make a left turn and go west on Oak Street crossing La Salle Street, continuing to Wells Street. Looking west and north, you can see Cabrini Green, Chicago's infamous public housing project and remembered as former Mayor Jane Byrne's temporary residence. In the late 1800s, the largest Swedish population outside of Sweden lived west of Wells Street between Chicago Avenue and Division Street. Make a left turn and go south on Wells Street taking it to Huron Street and the heart of the River North.

River North, roughly bordered by Chicago Avenue on the north, the Chicago river on the south and west, and Wells Street on the east, features many of Chicago's top art galleries. If interested wander through Chicago's "Suho," the local name for the Art Gallery district along Superior Street and Huron Street. Make a right turn and go west on Huron Street watching for the stop sign by the "El" tracks. Pass under the "El" and cross Orleans Street and enter the western section of River North. You have now traveled just under 3 miles from the starting point.

On the surface, this part of River North looks like the rustbelt Chicago of old, with aging commercial buildings, double parked trucks, vacant lots, and oddly the sweet smell of chocolate. Look a little closer and you'll see restaurants, art galleries, photography studios, and signs advertising loft space. At Kingsbury Street go left one block to Erie Street. Go left and east on Erie Street then make a small loop through River North. At Orleans Street go right for one block to Ontario Street and make a right turn. Continue west passing the Berghoff Restaurant and Brewery to Kingsbury Street. At Kingsbury Street go left and continue south to Kinzie Street. On your right is the popular and exclusive East Bank Health Club.

Go right on Kinzie and cross the Chicago river on the Kinzie Street bridge. It was just south of the Kinzie Street bridge and near the wooden pilings on the east side of the river where The Great Chicago Flood of 1992 began. An automobile size hole, in one of the tunnels, created when new pilings were being installed, sent 250 million gallons of water coursing through Chicago's 64-mile underground tunnel system. The flood waters filled subbasements of many office and retail businesses and also damaged miles of electric and fiber-optic lines running through the no-longer used freight tunnels. Over 200,000 people were evacuated from Chicago's Loop, subway lines were closed for weeks, and business losses were close to $1 billion. Though few people actually saw the flood waters, the insidious peril rekindled memories of Chicago's greatest natural disaster - the Great Chicago Fire of 1871.

Kinzie Street Bridge - Dan Broten

The area near the Kinzie Street bridge was originally home to Irish workers who were followed by Swedes and then later Italians. Since the 1920s, this vicinity has mainly housed commercial and light industry. Continue west on Kinzie Street to Clinton Street. Looking west, one block and on the right, is the Blommer Chocolate Company, the source of the sweet chocolate smell that fills the air. Chicago continues to be the largest candy manufacturing center in the United States. At Clinton Street go left (watch out for the railroad tracks). Follow Clinton south under the Lake Street "El" tracks to Randolph Street. Go right on Randolph Street and proceed west 1.2 miles to Union Park.

As you begin your westward ride on Randolph Street, you enter the old Haymarket Square market area. Running west, and including the stretch that now passes over the Kennedy Expressway, Haymarket Square was one of five market areas in Chicago in 1886. Poor immigrant workers, trying to stretch their meager salaries, came to the markets to buy directly from farmers. Haymarket Square was a bustling market area with numerous food stalls, carts, horses, fruit and vegetable stands, and hundreds of busy shoppers.

Haymarket Square is most famous for the police riot that occurred here during the turbulent 1880s. At that time Chicago was a hotbed for labor unrest, and on the evening of May 4, 1886, several thousand immigrant workers attended a labor meeting at the Haymarket Square. Near the end of the peaceful meeting, Chicago policemen marched into the square and began clubbing workers. Then, without warning, someone, still unknown to this day, tossed a bomb into the crowd killing several policemen and workers. Eight men, mostly German labor leaders, were eventually charged with conspiracy and found guilty. The strikes, protests, bombing and trial were symptomatic of Chicago's deep prejudice against immigrant workers and their perceived threat to the social order.

Continue west on Randolph Street and just over the Kennedy Expressway you'll enter a small market area.

Union Park and Jackson Boulevard Loop

Now begins the loop through Chicago's Near West Side to Union Park and the Jackson Boulevard Historic District. To shortcut this loop, take Halsted Street left and follow it south into Greektown. This shortcut saves 2.5 miles. For those following the designated route, ride the curb lanes of Randolph Street and proceed west to Union Park.

If interested you can detour to the Harpo Studios, home of The Oprah Winfrey Show. The studios are located one block south of Randolph Street on Carpenter Street and Washington Boulevard. A second optional detour is to the Museum of Holography located one block south of Randolph on May Street and Washington Boulevard.

The designated route continues west on Randolph Street. In the late 1800s, this section of the Near West Side was one of Chicago's premier residential neighborhoods. Union Park, at the western end of Randolph Street, was once one of Chicago's most beautiful parks with lagoons, gardens and rustic pedestrian bridges. Though the park no longer has ponds or boats it is still widely used. Going west of Ogden Avenue or north of Randolph Street is **not recommended.** Walk your bicycle along the east sidewalk of Ogden Avenue and go one block south to Washington Boulevard. Looking west, you can see the the Chicago Stadium, home of the Bulls and Blackhawks. Ashland Avenue runs north and south. This stretch is known as "Union Row, named for the many Union headquarters that line the street.

You will now begin to work your way one half mile to the Jackson Boulevard Historic District. Take Washington Boulevard east two blocks to Loomis Street. Go right and follow Loomis south past the slight jog at Madison Street to Monroe Street. Make a right on Monroe and head west with Skinner Park on your left. At the western end of the park, go left on Laflin Street for two blocks to Jackson Boulevard. Between Laflin Street and Ashland Avenue is the Jackson Boulevard Historic District. This small stretch of townhomes is all that remains of what was once the prosperous Near West Side residential neighborhood.

Leaving the Historic District, you will pedal one mile to Greektown at Jackson Boulevard and Halsted Street. On your left is Whitney Young High School and straight ahead, casting a long shadow in the early morning, is the 110-story Sears Tower. Further along at 1137 W. Jackson Boulevard is Fannie-May Candies.

At Jackson Boulevard and Halsted Street is Greektown. Lock your bicycle and wander along the west sidewalk of Halsted Street where most of the Greek restaurants and shops are located. Today's Greektown is just a small reminder of the once flourishing Greek community that grew up south of here at the turn of the century. At its peak in the 1930s and 1940s, more than 30,000 Greek immigrants lived and worked near Halsted Street and Harrison Street. Unfortunately, construction of the Eisenhower Expressway and the University of Illinois essentially destroyed the old Greek neighborhood. The restaurants and stores moved north of the Eisenhower Expressway where Greektown stands today. As the restaurant trade required little capital or prior experience, Greek immigrants soon flourished in this trade. Though Greektown is small and not an official "neighborhood" it preserves the sights, sounds, and most importantly the smells of Greek life. The total distance since the starting point is 7.1 miles.

Leaving Greektown, travel south on Halsted Street crossing the Eisenhower Expressway and continuing to Polk Street. At Polk Street and Halsted Street is the entrance to the University of Illinois at Chicago, and the Jane Addams Hull-House Museum. This entire area, including the current University of Illinois campus, was once the largest immigrant portal district is Chicago. Starting in the 1850s and 1860s, German, Irish, Bohemian, and French immigrants lived and worked in this general vicinity. As older immigrant groups assimilated and became more prosperous they moved on, and in their place came new immigrant groups to start the process over again. Starting in the 1890s Jewish, Italian, and Greek immigrants moved into the Near West Side. Today, the Maxwell Street Market, Little

Italy, and Greektown stand as mementos of those early days.

Into this neighborhood came two idealistic women, who, in 1899, established Hull-House, the first settlement house in Chicago and the most famous in the nation. Jane Addams and Ellen Gate Starr's Hull-House fought for child labor laws, encouraged unionization, sought equal pay for women, exposed government corruption, and provided education to Chicago's poorest immigrants. Jane Addams eventually won the Nobel prize for her efforts on behalf of Chicago's "huddled masses." Jane Addams Hull-House was declared a National Historic Landmark in 1967. Today, the museum has an extensive photo exhibit showing how this part of the city looked at the turn of the century.

The entrance to the University of Illinois at Chicago is just behind the Hull-House museum. Riding and exploring the campus adds approximately .5 mile to the trip total, but be sure to obey any posted bicycle riding regulations. The University of Illinois at Chicago began in 1946 as a two-year undergraduate division on Navy Pier, and has since grown to be the largest university in the Chicago area with over 25,000 students.

As you leave the University of Illinois at Chicago, proceed south on Halsted Street to the traffic light at Taylor Street. The Little Italy and West Side Medical Center Loop, begins and ends at this intersection of Taylor Street. Go right and follow Taylor Street west across Morgan Street and into the heart of Little Italy. Along Taylor Street, you'll find many Italian restaurants and grocery stores, along with Mario's, a local favorite for Italian Lemonade. Continue west on Taylor Street to Racine Avenue. Make a right and go north on Racine Avenue to Lexington Street. At the northwest corner of Taylor and Racine are the Jane Addams public housing projects. The influence of the University of Illinois can be seen by the proximity of these public housing projects to the expensive townhomes just across the street. At Lexington Avenue, go left and proceed west passing the attractive Arrigo Park all the way to Loomis Street. Just before Loomis Street, on your left, is a beautiful fountain and a excellent place to rest.

Temporarily leaving the residential neighborhood, you'll take a brief detour through the West Side Medical Center complex. Take Loomis Street left and go south returning to Taylor Street. At Taylor go right and proceed west through the commercial district of Little Italy and stop at Ashland Avenue.

West Side Medical Center Loop

To continue on the designated route, cross Ashland Avenue and continue west on Taylor Street to Wood Street. To shortcut the West Side Medical Center Loop, go right on Ashland and pedal to Harrison Street. At Wood Street make a right and go north to Harrison Street. At Harrison Street go right, continuing east past Ashland Avenue and returning to the more residential section of the Little Italy.

The West Side Medical Center is often referred to as the largest concentration of medical facilities in the world. Within this general area is the University of Illinois Hospital, Cook County Hospital, Rush-Presbyterian-St. Lukes Hospital, the Illinois State Psychiatric Institute, the Veterans Administration West Side Medical Center, Rush Medical University, and numerous medical offices.

Continue east on Harrison Street to Loomis Street and make a right turn. Follow Loomis Street south two blocks to Lexington Street. Go right on Lexington Street traveling west one block to Laflin Street. Make a right at Laflin Street and go one block north to Flournoy Street. Go right on Flournoy Street taking it east to Racine Avenue. Along Flournoy, Laflin, and Lexington Streets are many stately three-story greystones dating to the turn of the century. At 1336 W. Flournoy Street is the beautiful Notre Dame de Chicago church.

At Racine Avenue make a right and go south to Polk Street. Take Polk Street left and continue east into the old section of Little Italy. The corner of Polk and Carpenter has a simple charm with a couple of Italian fast food restaurants and grocery stores. At Miller

Street go right returning to Taylor Street. Take Taylor Street left and pedal east back to Halsted Street.

Maxwell Street Market Loop

To begin the .7 mile Maxwell Street Market Loop make a right on Halsted street and pedal south. To shortcut the Maxwell Street Market loop, continue east on Taylor Street. Maxwell Street is not the best part of town, so exercise caution and pedal with authority.

Traveling south on Halsted Street you pass the ballfields for the University of Illinois. Crossing Roosevelt Road (12th Street) you enter a somewhat rundown retail shopping district, and further south is the Maxwell Street Market. In the early part of this century, more than 15,000 Jewish immigrants lived and worked near the Maxwell Street Market. In those days, the market was a bustling place where many immigrants got their first jobs haggling in the market. Many older Chicagoans have fond memories of taking the streetcar to Maxwell Street on Sunday mornings. Unfortunately, Maxwell Street is not what it used to be. The University of Illinois has expansion plans which will lead to the demise of the Maxwell Street Market. You should not go further south than Maxwell Street. Return north on Halsted Street back to Taylor Street.

At Taylor Street and Halsted Street, you begin your 2.4 mile trip back to the starting point. Travel east on Taylor Street and cross over the recently reconstructed Dan Ryan Expressway. Just east of the expressway, on the southeast corner of Taylor Street and Jefferson Street, is the Chicago Fire Department Robert J. Quinn Fire Academy. On the Jefferson Street side of the Fire Academy is the "The Flame" statue which commemorates the site where on October 8, 1871 the Great Chicago Fire began. Starting in the rear of Mrs. O'Leary's barn at Dekoven Street and Jefferson Street, the fire burned for almost three days, completely destroying everything in its path. From this site the fire burned north four miles to Fullerton Avenue engulfing four square miles.

Continue east on Taylor Street one block to Clinton Street. Go right and take Clinton south to the traffic light at Roosevelt Road. Carefully cross Roosevelt Road and make a left to go east. Continue east on Roosevelt Road crossing over the Chicago River and the railroad yards with Chicago's new "fireproof" skyline on your left. Roosevelt Road ends at Michigan Avenue where you make a left and take the 11th Street pedestrian/bicycle bridge across the Illinois Central railroad tracks to Columbus Drive. Take the west Columbus Drive sidewalk bicycle route north to Balboa Drive. Cross Columbus Drive at the Balboa Drive traffic light and continue north on the east Columbus Drive sidewalk bicycle route all the way to the starting point at Monroe Drive and Columbus Drive.

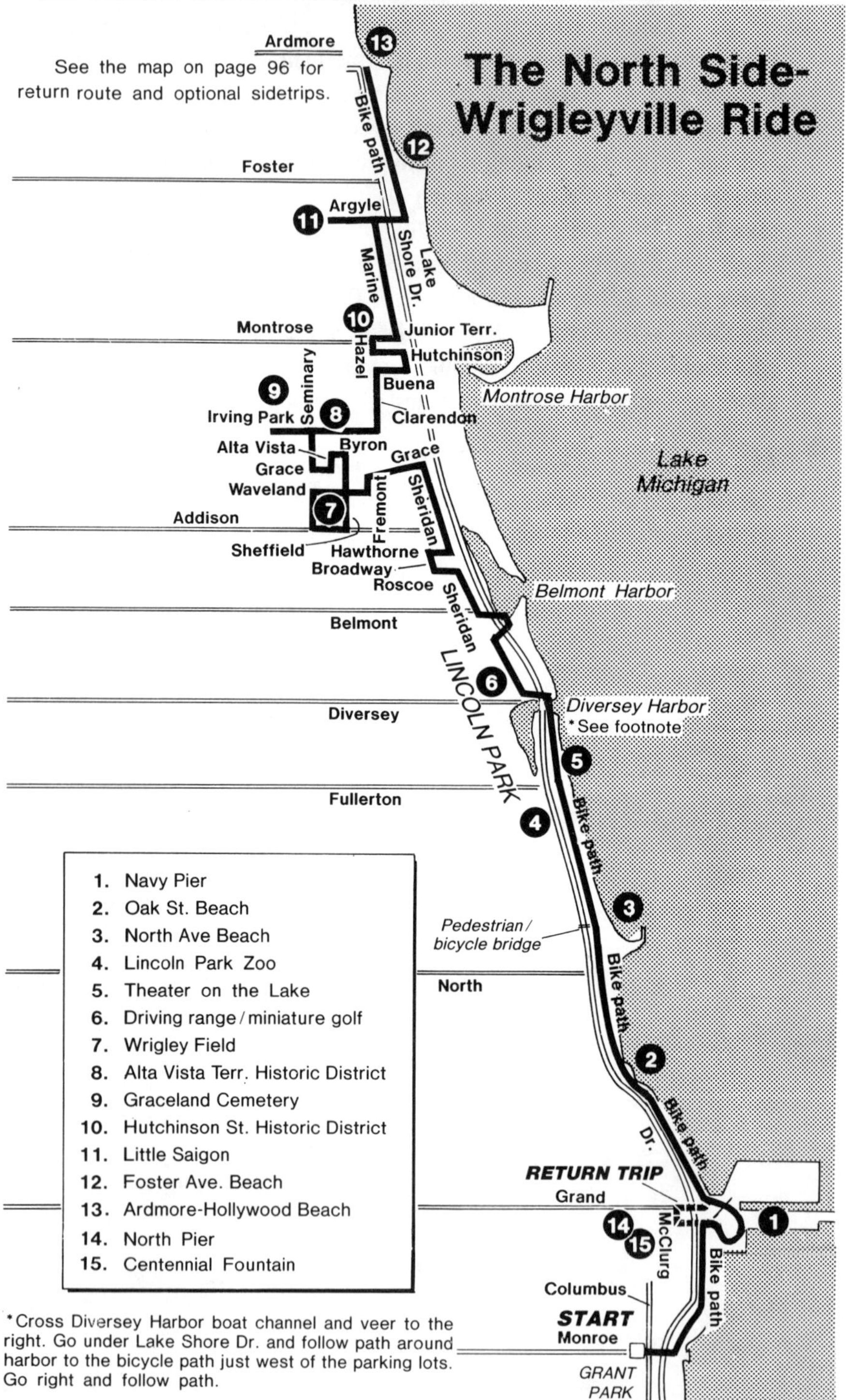
The North Side-Wrigleyville Ride
See the map on page 96 for return route and optional sidetrips.
Ardmore
Bike path
Foster
Argyle
Lake Shore Dr.
Marine
Montrose
Junior Terr.
Hutchinson
Hazel
Seminary
Buena
Montrose Harbor
Irving Park
Clarendon
Alta Vista
Byron
Grace
Grace
Waveland
Lake Michigan
Addison
Fremont
Sheridan
Sheffield
Hawthorne
Broadway
Roscoe
Belmont Harbor
Belmont
Sheridan
LINCOLN PARK
Diversey Harbor
*See footnote
Diversey
Fullerton
Bike path
Pedestrian/bicycle bridge
North
Bike path
Dr.
Bike path
RETURN TRIP
Grand
McClurg
Columbus
START
Monroe
GRANT PARK
Bike path
1. Navy Pier
2. Oak St. Beach
3. North Ave Beach
4. Lincoln Park Zoo
5. Theater on the Lake
6. Driving range/miniature golf
7. Wrigley Field
8. Alta Vista Terr. Historic District
9. Graceland Cemetery
10. Hutchinson St. Historic District
11. Little Saigon
12. Foster Ave. Beach
13. Ardmore-Hollywood Beach
14. North Pier
15. Centennial Fountain
*Cross Diversey Harbor boat channel and veer to the right. Go under Lake Shore Dr. and follow path around harbor to the bicycle path just west of the parking lots. Go right and follow path.

The North Side-Wrigleyville Ride

Start/End: Intersection of Columbus Drive and Monroe Drive

Distance: 25.6 miles (shortcuts reduce ride to 22.7 miles and optional sidetrips increase ride to 37.7 miles)

Time: 3 to 4 hours depending on sight-seeing and other stops

Difficulty/Safety: Moderate-to-strenuous distance
Light-to-moderate traffic

Shortcuts:

1. Skip Navy Pier Loop and save 1.2 miles.
2. Skip Little Saigon Loop and save .9 mile.
3. Skip North Pier Loop and save .8 mile.
4. Return south on Lakefront Bicycle Path at any point along route to cover desired distance.

Optional Sidetrips:

1. Graceland Cemetery - total 1.0 mile.
2. Loyola University - total 2.2 miles.
3. Northwestern University - total 12.1 miles.

Bicycle Shops:

Turin Bicycle
435 E. Illinois Street
(312) 923-0100

Kozy's Cyclery Fitness
3712 N. Halsted street
(312) 281-2263

Cycle Smithy
2468 N. Clark Street
(312) 281-0444

Turin Bicycle Evanston Ltd.
1027 Davis Street
Evanston, Il, 60201
(708) 864-7660

Activities/Highlights:

Navy Pier
Grand Avenue and Lake Michigan

Lincoln Park

- Lincoln Park Zoo
  Fullerton and Cannon Drive

- Theater On The Lake
  Fullerton Avenue at Lake Michigan

- Golf Driving Range and Miniature Golf
  Diversey Drive just west of Lake Shore Drive

- Sydney R. Marovitz Golf Course (Waveland Golf Course)
  Irving Park Road just east of Lake Shore Drive

Architectural Highlights

- Hawthorne Place

- Alta Vista Terrace

- Hutchinson Street

Wrigley Field - Home of the Chicago Cubs
Addison Street and Clark Street

Little Saigon
Argyle Street between Marine Drive and Broadway Avenue

North Pier
435 E. Illinois Street
Shopping arcade along with Expressways
Children's Museum (527-1000)
The Chicago Maritime Museum (836-4343).

Sidetrip Attractions

- Graceland Cemetery
  Irving Park Road and Clark Street

- Loyola University
  Sheridan Road and Devon Avenue

- Northwestern University
  Sheridan Road and South Campus Drive in Evanston

Dan Broten

Lakefront Bicycle Path at North Avenue - Dan Broten

The North Side-Wrigleyville Ride

Starts up north in Hollywood
Water on the driver's side
Concrete mountains rearin' up
Throwin' shadows just about 5
Sometimes you can feel the green
If your mind is feeling fine
Ain't no finer place to be
Than riding Lake Shore Drive

Aliota, Haynes and Jeremiah
"Lake Shore Drive," 1976

Most Chicagoans as well as many out of town visitors are familiar with Chicago's north lakefront park system. Lincoln Park's 1,200 acres, extending from Oak Street north almost six miles to Hollywood Avenue, provide an oasis of greenway amidst the asphalt laden city. On any summer weekend, thousands of visitors flock to Lincoln Park to enjoy the museums, ballfields, gardens, miles of sandy beaches, and world famous Lincoln Park Zoo.

The North Side-Wrigleyville Ride is designed to satisfy most cyclists desire to ride along the lakefront, and, at the same time, provide an interesting diversion into the neighborhoods that lie just west of the bicycle path. The designated route will take you northward to Navy Pier, along the Lakefront Bicycle Path past Oak Street Beach, North Avenue Beach, Fullerton Avenue Beach, and then inland to Wrigley Field.

Along the way you will pass through the high-rise lakefront condo districts that line Lake Shore Drive and into the neighborhoods of Lakeview, Wrigleyville, Buena Park, and Uptown. Within these neighborhoods you will pass three historic and architecturally significant streets that preserve the residential architecture of the late 19th century. The route will also take you into Little Saigon, Chicago's newest Asian shopping district. In addition, there are optional sidetrips to Graceland Cemetery, Loyola University, and Northwestern University. Finally, you will return along the Lakefront Bicycle Path stopping at North Pier and the Centennial Fountain.

The ride begins at Columbus Drive and Monroe Drive. Take the north sidewalk of Monroe Drive east and cross Lake Shore Drive at the traffic light. Make a left and pickup the Lakefront Bicycle Path and go north 1.2 miles to Navy Pier. On your right is Monroe Harbor and the Columbia Yacht Club. Continuing north you veer left and follow a slight incline up to the bridge across the Chicago River with the Chicago Fire Department Boat House and the locks of the Chicago River just below you.

The Chicago River - Dan Broten

As you cross over the river, head downhill towards the traffic light at Illinois Street. At the light, make a right turn and pedal east on Illinois Street to the entrance of Navy Pier at Grand Avenue and the lakefront. The route continues 1.3 miles to the tip of Navy Pier and back to the Lakefront Bicycle Path at Ohio Street.

Navy Pier, named for Navy veterans of World War I, opened in 1916 for freight handling and recreational activities. In 1946, Navy Pier was leased to the University of Illinois and used as an undergraduate division for returning veterans. By 1965, the west side campus of the University of Illinois had opened and the Navy Pier division was closed. During the 1970s and 1980s, Navy Pier was used for music and ethnic festivals and continues to serve several Lake Michigan tour boat operators. When completed in 1994, the $150 million Navy Pier renovation project promises to become one of Chicago's most popular tourist attractions.

When exiting Navy Pier, proceed to the right and follow the roadway to the Lakefront Bicycle Path at Ohio Street. On the way, you pass the Water Filtration Plant which filters drinking water for Chicago and its suburbs. Just west of the Filtration Plant is Olive Park which offers outstanding views of the skyline. Take the opportunity to explore Olive Park, returning to the designated route along Ohio Street.

Pickup the Lakefront Bicycle Path just west of the Ohio Street Beach and go right proceeding north one mile to Oak Street Beach. This concrete stretch of the Lakefront Bicycle Path is angled slightly downward toward the water line, and is an excellent place to ride hard and fast. On your right is "Outer Harbor," a popular mooring spot for sailboats on hot summer evenings. On your left is Lake Shore Drive with Chicago's "Magnificent Mile" just a few blocks further west along Michigan Avenue.

Slow down as you approach Oak Street Beach as this is one of Chicago's most popular beaches. The line of high-rises facing Lake Michigan and stretching north from Oak Street to North Avenue is Chicago's most affluent residential neighborhood - "The

Gold Coast." Rounding the bend, you approach North Avenue Beach, another popular beach. Follow the marked bicycle path **behind** the beach house.

Continue north on the Lakefront Bicycle Path .9 mile to Fullerton Parkway. About .1 mile north of the beach house is the pedestrian/bicycle bridge that crosses Lake Shore Drive into the heart of Lincoln Park. Please refer to the The Great Chicago Pizza Ride for highlights of Lincoln Park. The designated route takes you north along the bicycle path, passing the increasingly narrower sandy beaches of Fullerton Avenue Beach. The Theater On The Lake is located just north of Fullerton Parkway on the lakefront.

Continue north along the Lakefront Bicycle Path .6 mile to Diversey Harbor where you head inland. Use **caution** along this area since you will be sharing the narrow sidewalk with pedestrians. Follow the path to the left as you near the bridge that connects Diversey Harbor with Lake Michigan. Stay left and go over the bridge following the path to the right and **under** Lake Shore Drive. The Lakefront Bicycle Path continues north while you head inland. It is recommended that you **walk** along the path that takes you under Lake Shore Drive.

West of the tunnel is quaint Diversey Harbor with its charming views of Chicago's skyline. Stay on the path as it winds around the northern edge of the harbor. Just west of the parking lots, look for the bicycle/jogging path. Go right on the path and follow it north to the Lincoln Park Golf Driving Range and Miniature Golf. If you want to practice your driving or play Miniature Golf, lock your bicycle nearby, or, better yet, bring it into the driving range area.

Leave the Driving Range by continuing north on the inland bicycle path .6 mile to Belmont Avenue and Lake Shore Drive. Briefly follow the path as it winds through the greenways of Lincoln Park and passes under Lake Shore Drive where it joins with the Lakefront Bicycle Path. At the Belmont Avenue traffic light go left and travel under Lake Shore Drive. Then make a right turn onto northbound Sheridan Road/Marine Drive. Follow Sheridan Road/

Marine Drive three blocks north and make a left turn onto westbound Roscoe Street.

The designated route takes you through the eastern portion of the Lakeview neighborhood and to the Hawthorne Place Historic District. Take Roscoe Street west one block to Broadway Avenue. At Broadway Avenue, go right one block to Hawthorne Place and make another right turn. During the 1850s, the stage coach ran along Broadway Avenue (which was then known as Lake View Plank Road). The homes along Hawthorne Place recall a time when Lakeview was a lazy summer getaway from the hustle and bustle of "far away" Chicago.

Take Hawthorne Place east and make a left turn on Sheridan Road/Marine Drive heading north. Cross Addison Street and continue north to the traffic light at Grace Street. Go left onto westbound Grace Street past Broadway Avenue and Halsted Street to Freemont Street. At Freemont Street, make a left turn and go south two blocks to Waveland Avenue. As you make your right turn onto westbound Waveland Avenue, Wrigley Field appears in the distance with the gigantic "Chicago Cubs" sign behind the Howard "El" line tracks. Continue west on Waveland Avenue to Sheffield Avenue where you find the bleacher entrance to the ballpark. You have now traveled 8.9 miles from the starting point.

When Wrigley Field opened in 1914, it was known as Weeghman Park in honor of the owner of the Chicago Federals Baseball Club, which was part of the Federal League, a splinter league that had formed in 1914. In 1916, Charles Henry Weeghman consolidated his team with the Chicago Cubs Baseball Club. The "new" Chicago Cubs played their first game in the ballpark that same year. During the 1920s, William Wrigley Jr. (of chewing gum fame) purchased the Chicago Cubs and renamed the ballpark Wrigley Field. The ballpark itself, designed by Zachary Taylor Davis (who also designed the original Comiskey Park), is baseball's most traditional and beautiful, with ivy covered walls, natural grass, and close-to-the-action seating.

Clark Street in Lincoln Park - M. Palucki

Make a left onto southbound Sheffield Avenue and circle around the ballpark. On the southeast corner of Sheffield Avenue and Waveland Avenue is the ever popular Murphy's Bleachers Bar. The homes lining the east side of Sheffield Avenue have rooftop viewing decks with food service and bars. Circle the ballpark returning to the intersection of Waveland Avenue and Sheffield Avenue.

The route continues from Wrigley Field .3 mile to the Alta Vista Terrace Historic District. At Sheffield Avenue make a left turn and travel two blocks north to Byron Street. At Byron Street go left and travel west two blocks to Alta Vista Terrace. Alta Vista Terrace captures the essence of 19th century townhouse design. Known as "the street of the forty doors," Alta Vista Terrace was built between 1900 and 1904 by real estate developer S.E. Gross, and every townhouse on each side of the street is duplicated with only minor variations at the diagonally opposite end of the street.

Leave the historic district by making a right turn onto westbound Grace Street. Go to the corner and make a right turn onto Seminary Avenue. Take Seminary Avenue north along the small parkway to Irving Park Road.

Graceland Cemetery Loop

To follow the Graceland Cemetery sidetrip, go left on Irving Park Road to Clark Street. Graceland Cemetery is the final resting place for many of Chicago's original "movers and shakers," and among those buried here are Marshall Field, Philip D. Armour, George Pullman, and Potter Palmer. Bicycles are not allowed in the cemetery, but walking tours can be arranged through the Chicago Architectural Foundation.

The designated route then takes you along busy eastbound Irving Park Road (make a right turn off of Seminary Avenue) past Byron's Hot Dogs - voted the number one Hot Dog in Chicago. Continue east on Irving Park Road past the traffic lights at Sheridan Road and Broadway Avenue. At the Clarendon Avenue traffic light make a left and pedal north to Buena Avenue. Take Buena Avenue right one block to Marine Drive. Go left one block on Marine Drive and make another left onto westbound Hutchinson Street.

This historic neighborhood is known as Buena Park. The Hutchinson Street Historic District includes Hutchinson Street and neighboring Hazel Street, Junior Terrace, and Cullom Avenue. Preserved along these streets are residential styles from the 1880s through the 1920s. This famous section of Buena Park features Queen Anne, Richardsonian Romanesque, and Prairie School designs.

Leave the Hutchinson Historic District by going west on Hutchinson Street to Hazel Street and then north to Junior Terrace. Make a right on Junior Terrace and proceed east with a slight jog to the left along Clarendon Avenue. Junior Terrace ends at Marine Drive where you go left and head north to Little Saigon. Along Marine Drive are many high-rise condominiums and apartment complexes. Just a few blocks inland from these relatively affluent residences are the hard streets of Uptown. Uptown, once known for its "Bright Light District" of theaters, ballrooms, and nightclubs, reached its peak during the 1920s.

Little Saigon Loop

Continue following Marine Drive north past Montrose Avenue and Lawrence Avenue to Argyle Street. Make a left and follow Argyle Street to Broadway Avenue and then back again for a one-mile roundtrip. As you approach the commercial zone on the western end of Argyle Street the atmosphere is more Southeast Asian than Mid-Western United States. In recent years, this area has become a new immigrant portal district for newcomers from Korea, Thailand, Laos, Cambodia, and Vietnam.

Take Argyle Street east and cross Marine Drive, working your way along the sidewalks through Lincoln Park to the pedestrian/ bicycle tunnel under Lake Shore Drive. As you emerge on the east side of Lake Shore Drive you once again join the Lakefront Bicycle Path.

The designated route takes you left and north one mile along the marked bicycle path to the end of the path at Ardmore-Hollywood Beach. You may want to skip this portion and return south on the bicycle path.

Lincoln Park began as a cemetery near today's North Avenue, and by 1900, it had grown to cover more than 300 acres. Because of high land values park officials decided to extend Lincoln Park by building eastward into Lake Michigan. Using tons of landfill Lincoln Park was eventually extended all the way to Ardmore-Hollywood Beach and today encompasses over 1200 acres. Lake Shore Drive, also known as Outer Drive, was built during the 1930s and completed to Hollywood Avenue in the 1950s.

The Lakefront Bicycle Path ends at lovely Ardmore-Hollywood Beach. This beach is never crowded, though it is one of Chicago's most attractive. From the starting point, you have now traveled 14.6 miles.

Loyola and Northwestern Loop

Below is the suggested route for those interested in extending their trip to Loyola University in Rogers Park or Northwestern University in Evanston. The route passes through the residential neighborhood of East Rogers Park and into the stunning mansion district of Evanston. To follow the designated route skip the next section.

Follow the Lakefront Bicycle Path to its terminus at Ardmore Avenue. Make a left at Ardmore Avenue and cross Sheridan Road one block to Kenmore Avenue. Go right and take Kenmore Avenue north until it ends at Sheridan Road. Carefully cross to the north side of Sheridan Road. Just west of Kenmore Avenue (at Winthrop Avenue) is the entrance to Loyola University. Make a right to enter

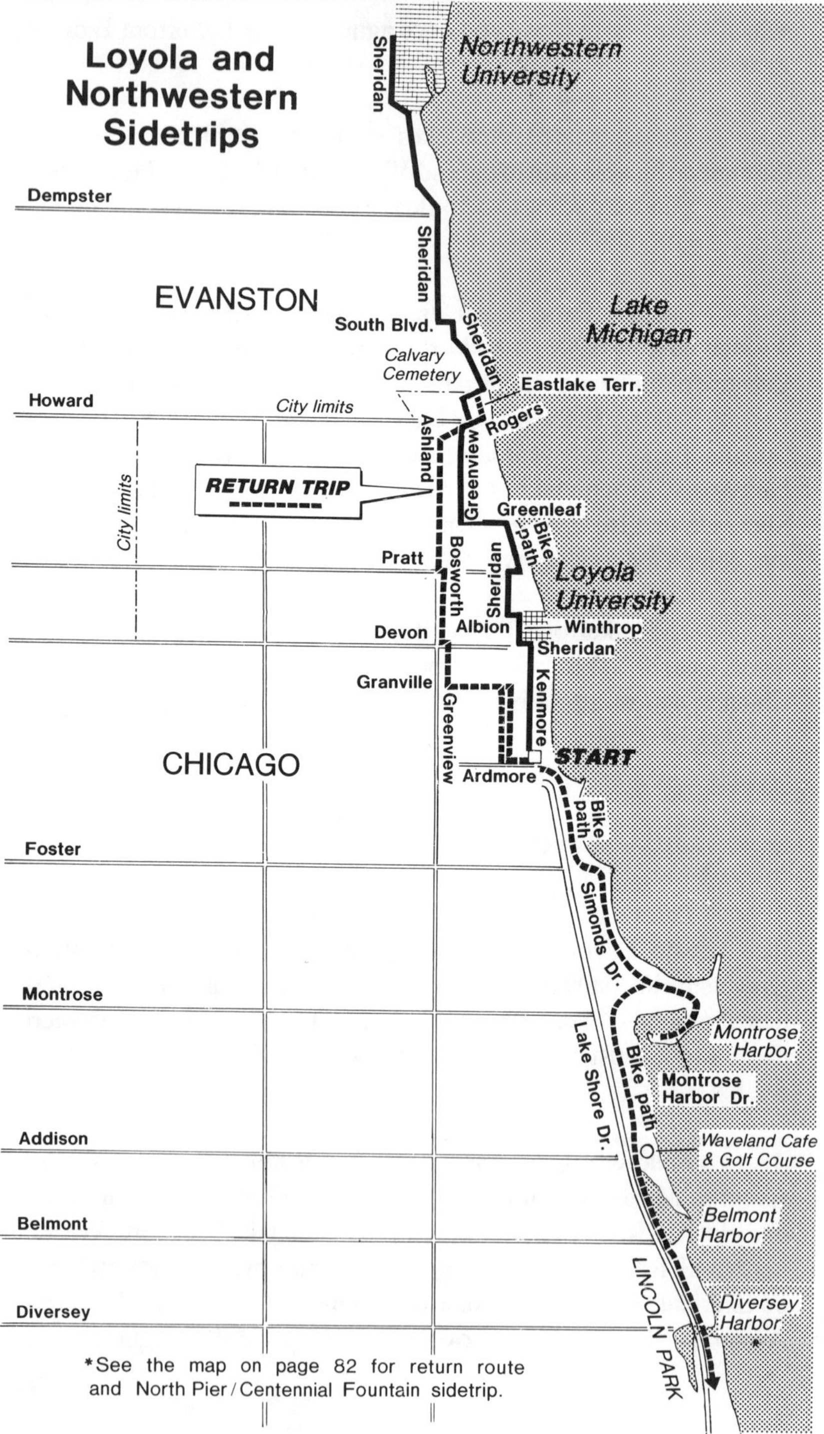
Loyola and Northwestern Sidetrips
Northwestern University
Sheridan
Dempster
Sheridan
EVANSTON
Lake Michigan
South Blvd.
Sheridan
Calvary Cemetery
Eastlake Terr.
Howard
City limits
Rogers
Ashland
Greenview
RETURN TRIP
City limits
Greenleaf
Bike path
Pratt
Bosworth
Sheridan
Loyola University
Devon
Albion
Winthrop
Sheridan
Granville
Kenmore
Greenview
CHICAGO
START
Ardmore
Bike path
Foster
Simonds Dr.
Montrose
Montrose Harbor
Lake Shore Dr.
Bike path
Montrose Harbor Dr.
Addison
Waveland Cafe & Golf Course
Belmont
Belmont Harbor
LINCOLN PARK
Diversey
Diversey Harbor
*See the map on page 82 for return route and North Pier/Centennial Fountain sidetrip.

the campus. To return south, retrace your way back to Sheridan Road and take Winthrop Avenue south back to Ardmore Avenue. Go left on Ardmore and pedal east across Sheridan Road where it connects with the Lakefront Bicycle Path. The total distance for the Loyola loop is 2.2 miles.

To continue on to Evanston, work your way through Loyola University looking for Winthrop Avenue on the north end of campus. Take Winthrop north a very short distance to Albion Avenue. Go left on Albion Avenue a short distance to Sheridan Road. These lovely single family homes are part of the East Rogers Park neighborhood. Make a right on Sheridan Road and go north four blocks, then make another right onto eastbound Pratt Avenue. Follow Pratt Avenue into Loyola Park and pick up the bicycle path taking it north through the park and past Loyola Beach. The bicycle path ends at Greenleaf Avenue where you go west crossing over Sheridan Road to Greenview Avenue. Go right on Greenview Avenue and pedal north to Rogers Avenue. Go right on Rogers and travel east to Sheridan Road. Make a left onto Sheridan Road and proceed north passing the Chicago city limits at Calvery Cemetery. Be sure to ride on the designated sidewalk bicycle route.

Sheridan Road can be confusing as it winds its way northward, but if you stay as close to Lake Michigan as possible, you can't get lost. Take some time to explore Evanston's beautiful lakefront parks just east of Sheridan Road. Northwestern University is at Sheridan Road and South Campus Drive. Visit the campus but be sure to pedal along the lakefront bicycle path just east of the campus.

When leaving Northwestern University follow Sheridan Road south. A sidetrip through downtown Evanston can be made by taking Clark Avenue west to Sherman Avenue. Follow Sherman Avenue left and south through downtown Evanston. Return to Sheridan Road by taking any side street east towards Lake Michigan.

Continue south on Sheridan Road past Calvery Cemetery (be sure to ride on the designated sidewalk bicycle route) and back into Chicago. The route back to the Lakefront Bicycle Path follows the marked City of Chicago bicycle route signs. At Rogers Avenue, make a right and travel west to Ashland Avenue. Make a left onto Ashland Avenue and continue south to Pratt Avenue. Go left on Pratt one block east to Bosworth Avenue. Make a right on Bosworth Avenue and take it south to Devon Avenue. Take Devon Avenue left one block to Greenview Avenue. Go right on Greenview Avenue and pedal south four blocks to Granville Avenue. Make a left on Granville Avenue and continue east to Winthrop Avenue. At Winthrop Avenue make a right turn and proceed south to Ardmore Avenue. Go left on Ardmore Avenue crossing over Sheridan Road and join up with the Lakefront Bicycle Path. Your total trip distance to Northwestern University and back is 12.1 miles.

North Avenue Beach House - Dan Broten

As you head south from Ardmore-Hollywood Beach follow the marked bicycle path to Foster Avenue Beach. From Foster Avenue Beach you have two choices for returning to the starting point. The fastest route is to continue south on the marked Lakefront Bicycle Path. Our designated route attempts to stay as close to the waters edge as possible, and is therefore more difficult and lengthy.

The roadway running parallel with Lake Michigan from Foster Avenue to Montrose Avenue is Simonds Drive. Take Simonds Drive left and south (watch out for cars backing out of the parking spaces). At Lawrence/Wilson Drive go left and continue south. About halfway between Foster Avenue Beach and Montrose-Wilson Avenue Beach is a man-made boat launching area.

Continue south on Lawrence/Wilson Drive to Simonds Drive. Go left on Simonds Drive and pedal south. On your right, is the highest point in Lincoln Park, Cricket Hill, which rises a "breathtaking" forty feet from the grassy fields below. Built of dirt from a tunnel excavation in 1948, Cricket Hill offers sledding, kite flying, and elevated viewing for local flatlanders. On any given Sunday, this section of Montrose Park could easily be mistaken for Chapultepec Park in Mexico City. Spanish music fills the air, as does the smell of carnitas and tacos from the many Mexican, Ecuadorian, Guatemalan, and Puerto Rican day-long fiestas. This park is the most colorful picnic area of all the lakefront parks with a truly foreign and exciting feeling.

Continue south on Simonds Drive to Montrose Harbor Drive. Go left on Montrose Harbor Drive and follow it to the tip of the Montrose Harbor peninsula. Montrose Harbor Drive, with its great views of Chicago's skyline, is also Chicago's most popular "lovers lane."

Return via the circle turnabout and take Montrose Harbor Drive as it bends northward around the Harbor where it finally intersects Montrose Drive. On your left is the Park Bait Shop which also sells snacks and soft drinks. Go left and follow Montrose Drive west to where the Lakefront Bicycle Path crosses near Lake Shore Drive.

The route then takes you south on the Lakefront Bicycle Path .8 mile to Brett's Waveland Cafe and Sydney R. Marovitz (Waveland) Golf Course. Follow the Lakefront Bicycle Path south along the western edge of the golf course. At the tennis courts veer left and follow the path as it winds its way to the Waveland Carillon and golf house, both built in 1931. Nearby is Brett's Waveland Cafe, which is considered to be the "best" concession stand in the park system. As you leave Brett's you pass a fenced-in Bird Sanctuary that offers refuge for hundreds of different bird species.

Continue along the Lakefront Bicycle Path just under one mile to the west end of Belmont Harbor. At the northern most point of Belmont Harbor and just off the bicycle path is an authentic red cedar Kwagulth Indian Totem Pole carved by British Colombian Indians. Continue south .7 mile to the Diversey Harbor boat channel. Just before crossing over the boat channel, go out to the tip of Diversey point for a excellent view of Chicago's skyline with the Theater on the Lake in the foreground. You have now returned to where you had earlier rode inland.

North Pier - M. Palucki

Proceed south 2.8 miles along the Lakefront Bicycle Path passing Fullerton Avenue Beach, North Avenue Beach, Oak Street Beach, all the way to the Grand Avenue just south of Ohio Street Beach. The designated route takes you off the bicycle path for a .8 mile roundtrip to North Pier and the Centennial Fountain. Take Grand Avenue to the right and west under Lake Shore Drive to McClurg Court. Go left on McClurg Court traveling south past Illinois Street. The North Pier Shopping Mall is on your left. Follow McClurg Court all the way until it ends at the Chicago River and The Centennial Fountain (one of Chicago's newest and nicest fountains). Take a few minutes to explore the surrounding area with its great views west along the Chicago river, and be sure to read the informative plaque on the fountain.

Return north on McClurg Court making a right onto the pedestrian walkway along the boat channel adjacent to North Pier. North Pier is a mixed-use shopping mall popular with both tourists and locals. If your interested lock your bicycle and wander into the mall.

Return to the designated route by taking McClurg Court north to Illinois Street. Go right on Illinois and take it east under Lake Shore Drive making a right onto the Lakefront Bicycle Path. Take the path south .8 mile to the traffic light at Monroe Drive and Lake Shore Drive. Cross on the north side of Monroe Drive and go one block west. You are now at the starting point at Monroe Drive and Columbus Drive.

Lakefront Bicycle Path at Diversey Harbor - Dan Broten

For More Information

There are several groups and clubs in Chicagoland that promote bicycle riding, sponsor organized rides, and provide information on cycling. Below are some of these groups and how they can be contacted:

The Chicagoland Bicycle Federation (CBF)
343 S. Dearborn Street, Suite 1017
Chicago, Il. 60604
312-42-PEDAL

Hostelling International - American Youth Hostels (AYH)
3036 N. Ashland Ave.
Chicago, Il. 60657
312-327-8114

The City of Chicago
Bureau of Traffic Engineering and Operations
320 N. Clark Street
Chicago, Il. 60610
312-744-4684
Call for free maps and bicycle safety pamphlet.

The Chicago Architecture Foundation
1800 S. Prairie Ave
Chicago, Il. 60616
312-922-3432
Call for a list of their organized tours.

Friends of the Parks
407 S. Dearborn Street
Chicago, Il. 60605
312-922-3307
Call for maps of Grant Park, Lincoln Park, and Jackson Park.

Recommended Reading

The Bike Bag Book by Tom Cuthbertson (Berkeley: Ten Speed Press, 1981) - Portable basic bicycle repair manual.

Bicycling Reference Book by The Bicycle Institute of America (1818 R Street NW, Washington, DC 20009 (202) 332-6986) - Excellent resource on all aspects of cycling.

Haymarket Revisited: A Tour Guide of Labor History Sites and Ethnic neighborhoods Connected with the Haymarket Affair by William Adelman (The Illinois Labor History Society, 28 E. Jackson Boulevard, Chicago, IL 60604 (312) 663-4107)

Chicago: City of Neighborhoods: Histories and Tours by Dominic A. Pacyga and Ellen Skerrett (Chicago Historical Society, 1601 N. Clark Street, Chicago, Il. 60614 (312) 642-4600)

Historic City - The Settlement of Chicago by the City of Chicago (Department of Development and Planning, Room 1000 - City Hall, Chicago, Il. 60602)

M. Palucki

Index

Bicycle Rentals

Erehwon Mountain Supply, 4
Turin Bicycles, 4
Village Cycle Center, 4

Bicycle Shops

Art's Cycle, 47
Buckingham Bike Shop, 27
Cycle Smithy, 27, 84
Erehwon Mountain Supply, 4
Irv's Bike Shop, 65
Kozy's Cyclery, 11, 83
Mt Chicago, 65
Quick Release Bike Shop, 27
Turin Bicycles, 47, 83
Turin Bicycle Evanston, 84
Village Cycle Center, 27, 65

Restaurants

Bacino's, 28,37
Bertucci's Corners, 17
Brett's Waveland Cafe, 100
Byron's Hot Dog Haus, 93
Cafe Brauer, 43
Edwardo's, 29, 38
Gino's East, 28,33
Giordano's, 28,35
Jimbo's Lounge, 18
Mario's Italian Lemonade, 78
Morrie O'Malley's, 22
O'Fame, 29, 38
Pippins, 34
Pizzeria Due, 28, 31, 32
Pizzeria Uno, 28, 31, 32
Ranalli's, 28, 35
Renaldi's, 29,41
Zum Deuchen Eck, 39

Sight-Seeing

Adler Planetarium, 48, 54
Alta Vista Terrace Historic District, 93
Armour Square neighborhood, 17
Arrigo Park, 78
Astor Street Historic District, 34

Bridgeport neighborhood, 20
Buckingham Fountain, 15
Buena Park neighborhood, 94
Burnham, Daniel H., 52

Centennial Fountain, 101
Chicago Academy of Sciences, 28, 43
Chicago Architectural Foundation, 48
Chicago Fire, 71, 80
Chicago Flood, 74
Chicago Historical Society, 28, 34
Chicago Maritime Museum, 85
Chinatown, 17
Comiskey Park, 18
Cornell, Paul, 56
Cricket Hill, 99

Dearborn Station, 24
DePaul University, 40
Du Sable Museum, 48, 60

Elks National Monument, 41
Expressways Children's Museum, 85

Field Museum, 47, 52

Gold Coast, 34
Graceland Cemetery, 93
Grant Park, 52

Index

Grant, Ulysses S., 44, 52
Greektown, 77

Harpo Studios, 76
Hawthorne Place, 91
Haymarket Square, 75
Here's Chicago, 33
Hull-House Museum, 66, 78
Hutchinson Street
Historic District, 94
Hyde Park neighborhood, 56

Jackson Boulevard
Historic District, 76
Jackson Park, 62
James C. Petrillo
Music Shell, 14
Japanese Garden, 62

Kenwood neighborhood, 57

Lakeview neighborhood, 39, 91
Lincoln Park, 34, 42, 87, 95
Lincoln Park Conservatory, 42
Lincoln Park neighborhood, 37
Lincoln Park Zoo, 42
Little Italy, 78
Little Saigon, 94
Loyola University, 95

Magnificent Mile, 33
Maxwell Street Market, 80
McCormick Place, 55
McCormick Row House
District, 40
Meigs Field, 54
Midway Plaisance, 59
Moore, Henry, Nuclear
Energy sculpture, 59
Museum of Holography, 66, 76
Museum of Science
and Industry, 48, 60

Navy Pier, 89
Newberry Library, 65, 73
New Town, 41
North Pier, 101
Northwestern University, 95

Ogden Mall, 36
Old Town, 35
Olive Park, 89
Oprah Winfrey Show, 76

Paul H. Douglas Nature
Sanctuary, 62
Prairie Avenue Historic
District, 11, 16

Robe House, 59
Rockefeller Chapel, 59
Rush Street Entertainment
District, 34

Saint-Gauden, Augustus,
Standing Lincoln sculpture, 34
Shedd Aquarium, 47,53
Sheffield Square
neighborhood, 38
Solidarity Drive, 54

Taft, Lorado, Fountain of
Time sculpture, 60

Union Stockyard Gate, 11, 21
University of Chicago, 57
University of Illinois
at Chicago, 78
Uptown, 94

Washington Square Park, 73
West Side Medical Center, 79
Wrigley Field, 91
Wooded Island, 62

About The Author

Michael Palucki is a longtime Chicagoan and avid cyclist. His travel and cycling adventures include trips to Europe, Africa, Australia, New Zealand, Southeast Asia, South America, and throughout the United States. In addition, Michael has taught history at area high schools and today writes travel articles as a free-lance writer. He recently relocated to Southern California where he is organizing historic bicycle tours of San Diego County. To receive a free bicycle tour brochure write to Pastime Publications.

BOOK ORDER FORM

CHICAGO BICYCLE GUIDEBOOK

Great Bicycle Riding Through Chicago's Lakefront Neighborhoods

Number of books:

Send to:
Name: ______________________________
Address: ______________________________
City: ________________ State: ___ Zip: ______

Book price:
$9.95
ISBN: 0-9634829-7-1

Shipping:
Book Rate: $1.75 for first book and 75 cents for each additional book

First Class: $3 per book

Payment: Send Check or Money Order
($9.95 plus shipping) payable to:

Pastime Publications
P.O. Box 3237
Seal Beach, California 90740-2237

Note: Please allow two to four weeks for delivery.
All orders must be prepaid.

MW01623018